To Philip
As we walk to
our place of
resurrection

BGE

Taking a Walk with Whitehead

(on aprl 2023)

Meditations with Process-Relational Theology

Bruce G. Epperly

Energion Publications
Gonzalez, Florida
2023

Copyright © 2023, Bruce Epperly

Unless otherwise noted, Scripture quotations are from New Revised Standard Version Bible, copyright © 1989 National Council of the Churches of Christ in the United States of America. Used by permission. All rights reserved worldwide.

Energion Publications
P. O. Box 841
Gonzalez, FL 32560

(850) 525-3916
pubs@energion.com

TABLE OF CONTENTS

CHAPTER ONE

IT WILL BE SOLVED IN THE WALKING

Movement is at the heart of theological and philosophical inspiration. When your body moves, your spirit moves as well. New ideas and emotions emerge. Unexpected vistas greet your eyes. Walls are torn down. Blockages removed. With movement, we discover new perspectives, whether walking on the beach, strolling with your dog in the neighborhood, hiking the Appalachian Trail or Muir Woods, or sauntering on unfamiliar boulevards in Manhattan, Paris, Washington DC, or London. The great New England walker, Henry David Thoreau asserted, "I cannot preserve my health and spirits, unless I spend four hours a day at least—and it is commonly more than that—sauntering through the woods and over the hills and fields, absolutely free from all worldly engagements." The naturalist-adventurer saw walking as the "greatest enterprise and adventure of the day." Movement promotes health of mind, body, and spirit. Movement may even improve relationships: when we are walking with a companion, trying to solve a problem or resolve a disagreement, it is difficult to stay stuck in rigid viewpoints. Movement can change attitudes as well as latitudes!

Transformation occurs when we lace up our shoes and hit the trail, walking through a familiar urban neighborhood, hiking through the woods, or meandering along the beach. Walking and spiritual transfiguration are companions. Abraham and Sarah receive God's blessing and the commission to go forth to a new land on foot and camel. On the first Easter day, two disciples overwhelmed by grief, encounter a stranger on the road to Emmaus, engage him in conversation, invite the stranger to supper, and then discover the Risen Jesus in the breaking of the bread. Jesus and Socrates walk the lanes of Galilee and Athens, respectively, embracing the synchronicity of roadside encounters from which healing and truth emerge.

Among the Greeks, there is a humorous account of the peripatetic Thales of Miletus (620-546 BCE), one of the first of the Pre-Socratic philosophers. Walking alone at night, captivated by the stars above, Thales fell into a well, demonstrating to scoffers the dangers of philosophical thinking. Another tale describes Thales gazing at the heavens, noticing the movements of the stars, and discerning that the year ahead would bring a bumper crop of olives. The philosopher, revealing the utility of philosophy, purchased all the olive presses in Greece, and watched the money pour in.

A dear friend, knowing that walking is at the heart of my intellectual and spiritual life, sent me a crystal paperweight, with the inscription *Solvitur Ambulando,* "it will be solved in the walking." In our time, the great Jewish theologian Abraham Joshua Heschel described marching with Martin Luther King with the words, "I felt like my legs were praying."

Process-relational theology, grounded in the philosophy of Alfred North Whitehead (1861-1947), is a theology of movement. The process is the reality. The whole universe and its Creator are in constant movement. All things flow, as the Pre-Socratic philosopher Heraclitus observed, and those who go with the flow, embracing the movements of their cells and souls, discover everlasting life within movement and change. As Whitehead notes, the world emerges and evolves from the interplay of change and permanence, revealed in the hymn:

> Abide with me
> Fast falls the eventide.

While we treasure the eternal and unchanging elements of life, we also experience the passing of time, all too quickly, as we live through summer days and winter evenings, the seasons of our lives, and the rise and fall of nations. Life is a perpetual perishing in which creative transformation gives birth to novelty, born from the impact of the past, and leaning toward future adventures. God's aim at wholeness propels us toward far horizons of spiritual adventure, joining transition and change with stability and everlasting life

Movement is metaphysical and mystical. Sprinting and jogging can be transformational. Swimming and dancing can energize our spirits. But, walking, perhaps more than any form of movement, combines familiarity and change, rest and action, and reflection and restlessness. When our legs are praying, we become a sounding board for the universe, awakening to inspiration and intuition and cleansing our senses and spirits to perceive messages along the pathway, inviting us to new ways of looking at ourselves and others. Walking invites us to contemplation and creativity, to opening to new ideas and intuitions flowing in and through us with every step.

This book was born on a walk. During a chill winter saunter near my home on Cape Cod, a phrase came to me: "Walking and Whitehead" and with it, a question, "What would emerge if I took my fifty years of studying process-relational theology on a daily spiritual-theological walk? What new ideas might emerge through this interplay of walking prayer and sauntering theology?" As I continued my predawn walk, I intuited a methodology for seeing process-relational theology and Whitehead's cosmology in a new way. I would immerse myself in Whitehead's North American writings, ranging from *Science and the Modern World* to his final essays, "Mathematics and the Good" and "Immortality." I would reflect on a short paragraph from Whitehead's writings on my early morning beach and neighborhood walks, stretching from Craigville and Covell's Beaches, and then often through the picturesque Craigville hamlet and West Hyannis Beach and Long Beach. Along the way, I would breathe deeply these paragraphs, opening my senses to the beauty and wonder of the place, letting my mind wander and images and words emerge, trusting divine inspiration along with my own creativity to bring forth insights into process-relational theology.

I imagined this to be a living, breathing project in what I've come to describe as "theo-spirituality," the integration of theological and philosophical visions with spiritual practices and mystical experiences. Making our theology and philosophy come alive, shaping how we experience the world. In my mind, both theology and philosophy begin in wonder and radical amazement, as Abraham Joshua Heschel avers, and then out of that wonder and amazement come words, images, and creeds. My goal in the walking was not to construct a scholastic systematic theology, and be confined to literal interpretations of Whitehead's words, add another volume to Whiteheadian theological and philosophical scholarship, or to present another introduction to process theology, but to join the intellect, intuition, imagination, and spirituality to plumb the depths of process-relational theology from the vantage point of a Cape Cod beach and the surrounding planet in the era of protest and pandemic.[1] My wonderings and wanderings would give birth to reflections on a North American mystical theology and a global and pluralistic vision of theological and philosophical reflection.

I trusted my fifty years of reading Whitehead and process theology to be the dynamic catalyst of revelation. I trusted text and experience to help me "live" process-theology on my walks and during the day. As I noted earlier, my process was simple: after re-reading the corpus of Whitehead's North American publications, I chose thirty passages from Whitehead's work to be the catalysts for prayerful writing. Each night before retiring, I would meditate on the passage for the following morning and then take the passage to bed with me, letting divine aims flow through the land of "sighs too deep for words." In the morning, I would meditate on the passage again, and then set out on a walk. Returning home, I would note my insights. I would devote a few days to each passage, though a few of my meditations came as graceful inspirations in just one morning. I would intuitively describe process-relational theology in the real time in which we live, occasionally noting the "headline news" of the day or the personal, national, and global crises we

---

1   I have written two introductions to process-relational theology: *Process Theology: A Guide for the Perplexed* (London: Bloomsbury/Continuum, 2011) and *Process Theology: Embracing Adventure with God* (Gonzales, FL: Energion, 2014).

face as the material for process-relational reflection. I followed this practice twice over the four month period from New Year's Day to early April 2021.

As I began the walk with Whitehead, I anticipated stability in my personal and professional life, amid a world of change. But in my peregrinations, I realized that I was once again on the edge of personal and relational adventure. Contemplating leaving my beloved Cape Cod to sojourn in the Washington DC area to be near our son and his family, I felt the need to let the insights of process-relational theology flow through me. Just as a process-relational theology began to shape my world view and decision-making as a college sophomore in the early 1970s, I needed process-relational insights to prepare for my next pilgrimage in which my wife and I would be uprooting, like Sarah and Abraham, to go from a place of beauty to the bustling promised land of the USA Capitol. Likely this move would involve my retirement from full-time ministry as well as a new home and new spiritual and vocational opportunities. I wanted to claim this space and time as sacred and as a catalyst for further walking adventures along the Potomac towpath and the highways and byways of suburban Maryland.

We are all on an adventure. The adventure of the day, the adventure of this season of life, never fully knowing the next step but living with hope for insight, inspiration, intuition, and grace and courage for the path ahead. An adventure of ideas emerging with each new day and season of life. As Thoreau counseled to walkers in all times and places: "We should go forth on the shortest walk, perchance, in the spirit of undying adventure, never to return; prepared to send back our embalmed hearts only, as relics to our desolate kingdoms. If you are ready to leave father and mother, and brother and sister, and wife and child and friends, and never see them again; if you have paid your debts, and made your will, and settled all your affairs, and are a free man; then you are ready for a walk."

Let us take walk with Whitehead. Let us learn as we walk along. Let us be peripatetic process-relational theologians, every step and breath a prayer. Every reflection an adventure of ideas. *Solvitur Ambulando,* "it will be solved in the walking."

Thankful in the Walking. As I wonder as I wander with Whitehead as my companion, I am grateful for my eight years as pastor of South Congregational Church, United Church of Christ, and their affirmation of my writing and teaching ministry. We have walked together in expanding the circles of ministry, joining theology, spirituality, hospitality, and social concern. I am grateful to my wife Kate with whom I have been walking, and sometimes meandering, since we first met in 1978. I am grateful for walks on Cape Cod beaches with my son and his family, and gallops with our Golden Doodle Tucker. I am especially thankful to my father Everett Lewis Epperly, Baptist pastor and faithful father, with whom I took many walks during my college and young adult years, sharing wisdom and enjoying the journey. I give thanks for my colleagues, students, and parishioners of over forty years and my gracious publisher Henry Neufeld and editor Chris Eyre. *Ubuntu,* "I am because of you."

The Path Ahead. As we begin our wanderings, our walk with Whitehead will be enhanced by exploring the contours of Alfred North Whitehead's life, philosophical background, and spiritual orientation. In the process of our sojourn, we will discover the spiritual and theological resources of Whitehead's thought. As we turn to the next chapter, let us wonder as we wander underneath the wide sky.

Chapter Two

WHITEHEAD'S
METAPHYSICAL MYSTICISM[2]

Alfred North Whitehead once asserted that the European philosophical tradition could be described as a series of footnotes to Plato, whose reflections remain a goldmine for philosophical and theological adventurers. The greatest of Western philosophers Plato (427-347 BCE) affirmed that the philosophical journey, the love of wisdom, begins in wonder. In a dialogue with a young Athenian Theaetetus, Socrates, described as the wisest of humans, notes: "I see my dear Theaetetus, that Theodorus had a true insight into your nature when he said that you were a philosopher, for wonder is the feeling of the philosopher, and philosophy begins in wonder." (Theaetetus 155 c-d, Jowett, translation) One might add that theology and spirituality also begin in wonder, the feeling of amazement or astonishment at the world in which we live and the Reality that gives life to all things.

Wonder inspires spiritual experience and theological reflection. The Psalmist captures the experience of wonder when he considers the majesty of God's creation and the incredible finite-infinity of humankind.

> O LORD, our Sovereign,
>   how majestic is your name in all the earth!
> You have set your glory above the heavens.
> Out of the mouths of babes and infants
> you have founded a bulwark because of your foes,
> to silence the enemy and the avenger.
> When I look at your heavens, the work of your fingers,

---

2   This chapter is based on a lecture for my "Month with a Mystic" class at South Congregational Church, United Church of Christ, Centerville, MA.

the moon and the stars that you have established;
what are human beings that you are mindful of them,
mortals that you care for them?
Yet you have made them a little lower than God,
    and crowned them with glory and honor. (Psalm 8:1-5)

In the long distant past, humans looked at the heavens in
amazement and perplexity, marveling at the very nature of life
itself and asking, first, why there is something rather than nothing
and then what endures in a world of perpetual perishing? They
pondered the reality of our short lifespan and finitude against the
backdrop of a Mystery beyond their imaginations. In rare moments, they were invited into the depths of life itself, where our
hearts beat with the Heartbeat of the Universe – Lao Tzu wandering aimlessly across China, experiencing the flow of life within
and beyond him; the Vedic sages discovering the divine vibratory
Word energizing the universe and inspiring the mystic quest; Moses confronted by a burning bush on the way to work and hearing
God's call to liberate his people; Buddha, meditating under the Bo
Tree and experiencing liberation from the round of aging, death,
and rebirth; and Socrates in rapt attention at the complexities of
human experience and then discovering that humility is the key to
wisdom. Their wisdom charted the universe within and inspired
them to explore the Mystery that gives birth to cosmic creation.

The spiritual child of the prophets, Jesus recognized the significance of wonder, when he joined intellectual, spiritual, and
emotional loves of God, with ethical behavior:

"You shall love the Lord your God with all your heart, and
with all your soul, and with all your mind." This is the greatest
and first commandment. And a second is like it: "You shall love
your neighbor as yourself." On these two commandments hang
all the law and the prophets. (Matthew 22:37-39)

Loving God with the mind is a form of worship. Study can be
a form of prayer. Theological and philosophical reflection can be
contemplative and inspirational. Intellectual challenges can purify

our doctrines and ethical systems, reminding us as did the Apostle Paul in Socratic fashion that "we have this treasure in clay jars, so that it may be made clear that this extraordinary power belongs to God and does not come from us." (2 Corinthians 4:7)

While some of the greatest mystics were simple souls, experiencing the pure love of God as the ultimate reality flowing through all life, other mystics sought to join mind and spirit in responding God's life-transforming and transcending presence in their lives. In the West, we find this marriage of mind and spirit enlivening the messages of Plato and Pythagoras, Plotinus and Augustine, Pelagius and Pascal, Hildegard and Julian, Schweitzer and Hammarskjold, and Thurman and Weil. We discover the interplay of mysticism, theological and moral reflection, and social transformation, in the law giver Moses and the prophetic activist Amos. We discern this interplay of intellect and mysticism in the Dalai Lama, Thomas Merton, Dorothee Sölle, Black Elk, Howard Thurman, Dorothy Day, Mother Teresa, and Thich Nhat Hanh. Mystics can be philosophers and philosophers can be mystics.

Whitehead's Journey. Generality of thought, the joining of the intimate with the Infinite, is at the heart of the philosophical journey, according to Alfred North Whitehead. In a philosophical adventure extending over six decades, Alfred North Whitehead incarnated the intellectual stature we identify with the quest for wisdom found among philosophers and mystics. Born in Ramsgate, England, in 1861, the son of an Anglican minister and school master of the Chatham House Academy, established by Whitehead's grandfather, Whitehead had from an early age a proclivity for mathematics and the sciences, studied mathematics at Trinity College, Cambridge, and taught at Trinity College from 1884-1910. During that time, he started his collaboration with his former student Bertrand Russell, to produce the three-volume text on the foundations of mathematics and symbolic logic, *Principia Mathematica*, published between 1910 and 1913.

For a period of eight years at Cambridge, Whitehead took a great interest in theology. Conversation companion Lucien Price notes that:

> This was all extracurricular, but so thorough that he amassed a sizable theological library. He dismissed the subject and sold the books. A Cambridge bookseller was willing to give quite a handsome figure for the collection. It then appeared that the pay must be taken in books at his shop. So he went on an orgy of book-buying until he had overdrawn his account.[3]

Although Whitehead took a hiatus from theological reflection, he returned to more explicit theological, cosmological, and spiritual reflection when he emigrated to the United States in his sixties to teach at Harvard University. Whitehead's world view and approach to truth was shaped by the collapse in the early twentieth century of Newtonian physics, which had been presumed to be the final word in the describing the universe. As Whitehead notes:

> I have been fooled once and I'll be damned if I'll be fooled again! Einstein is supposed to have made an epochal discovery [demolishing Newtonian certainty]. I am respectful and interested but also skeptical. There is no more reason to expect that Einstein's relativity is anything final, than Newton's *Principia*. The danger is dogmatic thought; it plays the devil with religion; and science is not immune from it.[4]

Whitehead's experience of disillusionment inspired him to focus on adventure and novelty as essential to the practices of religion, philosophy, and science, and the flourishing of civilization. Commitment to the "adventure of ideas" enlivens our intellectual and spiritual quests and invites us to explore new images of God and the world.

At age fifty, there were signs that Whitehead was reclaiming his prior interest in philosophy and religion. In 1911, Whitehead

---

3   Lucien Price, *Dialogues with Alfred North Whitehead* (Boston: Little, Brown and Company, 1954), 9.
4   Ibid., 345-346.

began a twelve-year stint holding professorial and administrative posts at the University of London, where he began to take serious interest in philosophy. The death of his son Eric, as well as the loss of a generation of young men, many of whom were his students, during World War I may have inspired the mathematician to seek the consolations of metaphysics and religion, the quest for something eternal in our perpetually perishing world.

In 1924, Whitehead was invited to join the faculty of Harvard University, where he taught in the philosophy department until 1937. As a professor at Harvard, Whitehead was set free to speculate on metaphysics, intellectual history, and religious experience grounded in his holistic vision of a philosophy of organism. The philosopher died in 1947, leaving a legacy that gave birth to process-relational theology and philosophy.

The Spirit of Philosophical Mysticism. In the spirit of Plato, Whitehead saw philosophy as a "voyage toward larger generalities" and asserted that "morality of outlook is conjoined with generality of outlook."[5] Unlike many philosophers of his time and our own, Whitehead saw speculative philosophy joining religion as well as science and linguistic analysis in our understanding of the universe. Philosophy must take religious experience seriously in its "wedding of imagination and common sense."[6] In words applicable to mystics throughout the ages, Whitehead asserts that "religion is the ultimate craving to infuse into the insistent particularity of emotion that nontemporal generality which primarily belongs to conceptual thought alone."[7] In many ways, the mystic's understanding of their experience resembles Whitehead's description of metaphysical discovery as similar to the flight of an airplane. "It starts from the ground of particular observation; it makes the flight into the thin

---

5   Alfred North Whitehead, *Process and Reality: Corrected Edition* (New York: Free Press, 1978), 10, 15.

6   Ibid., 17.

7   Ibid., 16.

air of imaginative generalization; and it again lands for renewed observation rendered acute by rational interpretation."[8]

Mystics are touched by the Holy, often while going about their daily lives, for example, in Moses' and Isaiah's encounters with God. Biblical mystics hear the voice of God speaking through a burning bush on the way to work or revealed in the experience of divine majesty at prayer time in the Jerusalem Temple, and then must live out their experiences of the Holy in the maelstrom of public life, whether liberating their people, challenging the social and religious practices of a nation gone astray, providing hope after catastrophe, or encountering God in the least of these with Mother Teresa on the Calcutta streets or Dorothy Day in urban soup kitchens. Heavenly experiences, universality wedded with intensity of feeling and thought, become catalysts for transforming the world.

Whitehead identifies mysticism with our experience of infinity in finite and fallible human experience. Theological reflection leads us to create something long-lasting out of the mystical experience, something that will save its immediacy or impact, or at least the memory of self-transcendence in our personal lives and communities. Words can't convey mystical experiences, except feebly; we are aware of having been in communication with infinitude and we know that no finite form can claim finality and orthodoxy for what is ultimately dynamic and transformative. The love of wisdom pushes us beyond static doctrine to concrete experiences of life in its dynamic and adventurous interdependence. Experience transforms theology and philosophy, and philosophy and theology shape our experiences.

In the next sections, I will describe key elements in Whitehead's metaphysical mysticism as it joins experience and theological reflection.

Wondering and Wandering Whitehead's Metaphysical Mysticism. German liberation theologian Dorothee Sölle asserts that we are all mystics. A few decades earlier philosopher-activist Simone Weil described the need for novel forms of mysticism appropriate to

---

8   Ibid., 5.

our time. According to Weil, we need saints and mystics whose spiritual experiences awaken them to the cries of the poor and the realities of injustice:

> Today it is not merely enough to be a saint, but we must have the saintliness demanded by the present moment, a new saintliness without precedent... A new type of sanctity is indeed a fresh spring, an invention. If all is kept in proportion and if the order of each thing is preserved, it is almost equivalent to a new revelation of the universe and of human destiny. It is the exposure of a large portion of truth and beauty hitherto concealed under a thick layer of dust.[9]

Whitehead charts a novel vision of mysticism, inspiring saints for our time, joining mind, body, and spirit, generality of thought, intuition, self-transcendence, and empathic connection with all creation. Whitehead's metaphysical mysticism challenges otherworldly, disembodied, individualistic, and anthropocentric images of the spiritual adventure. Our spiritual journeys involve loving God with heart, mind, and hands and claiming our vocation as God's companions in healing the earth. Whitehead's commitment to generality of thought inspires us to embrace a spirituality of stature, big enough to chart the universe and focused enough to see infinity in a grain of sand, described by process theologian Bernard Loomer:

> By size I mean the stature of a person's soul, the range and depth of his love, his capacity for relationships. I mean the volume of life you can take into your being and still maintain your integrity and individuality, the intensity and variety of outlook you can entertain in the unity of your being without feeling defensive or insecure. I mean the strength of your spirit to encourage others to become freer in the development of their diversity and uniqueness.[10]

---

9   Simone Weil, *Waiting for God* (New York: Harper Collins, 2009), 51.
10   Bernard Loomer, "S-I-Z-E is the Measure," Henry James Cargas and Bernard Lee, *Religious Experiences and Process Theology* (Mahweh, NJ: Paulist Press, 1976), 70.

Saints and mystics in our time must be large spirited, joining the wisdom of their own religious tradition with willingness
to challenge past certainties, learn from other wisdom traditions,
and seek to promote God's vision in everyday life and political
decision-making.

Relational Spirituality. According to Whitehead, the whole
universe conspires to create each moment of experience. Although
the philosopher asserts that spiritual growth requires solitude,
which gives birth to self-transcendence and global spirituality, our
lives are through and through social. We are linked to gather in
an intricate web of relatedness, in which, as Martin Luther King,
who was likely familiar with process theology, asserts: "For some
strange reason I cannot be what I ought to be until you are what
you ought to be. And you can never be what you ought to be until
I am what I ought to be. That's the way God's universe is made."[11]

Mysticism is about holy relatedness, experiencing ourselves in
lively unity with a dynamic universe. Growth in empathy characterizes the spiritual journey. The largeness of spirit characteristic of
mystical experience is grounded in the recognition that the universe
flows in and through us, and that the pain and joy of others is also
our pain.

In contrast to philosophical visions of an apathetic God who
observes us from a distance and for whom any contact with the
world of change is a fall from perfection, Whitehead sees God
in terms of empathetic companionship. God is known by God's
relationships with each individual creature as well as the entire
historical process. God is, as Whitehead avers, the fellow sufferer
who understands. God is also the loving companion who rejoices.
God is enriched in God's encounters with the world. New divine
experiences open new novel possibilities for God's presence in the
world. The divine pathos, as Abraham Joshua Heschel asserts, reflects God's intimate relatedness to cells as well as souls, and to
economics as well as monastics. In speaking of Israel's prophetic

---

11   Martin Luther King, *A Knock at Midnight, Midnight* (New York: Warner
     Books, 1978), 208.

spirituality, Heschel asserts that in contrast to Aristotle's apathetic and unchanging God, divine pathos denotes:

> Not an idea of goodness, but a loving care; not an immutable example, but an ongoing challenge, a dynamic relation between God and man....God is concerned about the world and shares in its fate. Indeed, this is the essence of God's moral nature; God's willingness to be intimately involved in the history of man.[12]

God and the world are intimately connected. An empathetic God fosters an empathetic spirituality. Mature spirituality is about imitating God and becoming like the God we revere. God plunges into the maelstrom of interdependence, and mystical experiences inspire us to do likewise. The Heart of the Universe embraces each moment's joy and sorrow, receiving as well as giving to bring beauty and Shalom our world. A spirituality of relatedness reminds us, in the words of Thomas Merton, that we are all guilty bystanders connected with our human and non-human siblings, whether we experience life from a Trappist monastery in Kentucky, a beach on Cape Cod, a school yard in Washington DC or London, England, or a retirement community in Claremont, California. Open to the world in its tragic beauty, our spirits grow as we embrace the beauty and ugliness of life, making it our own, growing in wisdom and stature, and inspired to become empathetic and large-souled companions in God's journey of creative-responsive love.

Enchanted Reality. Whitehead invites us to a world of praise and wonder. The heavens declare the glory of God and so do the cells of our bodies. Nature is alive, regardless of whether humans experience the non-human world. The universe pulsates with experience and creativity. The lifeless and disenchanted world described by materialists, mechanists, and dualists, gives way to a lively, re-enchanted world in which there are thin places everywhere. "The

---

12 Abraham Joshua Heschel, *The Prophets* (Peabody, MA: Hendrickson Publishers, 1962), Volume 2, 4-5.

world lives by its incarnation of God in itself."[13] All creatures are words of God and the whole earth, as Isaiah's angelic companions proclaim, is full of God's glory. (see Isaiah 6:1-8) Each moment of experience, human and non-alike, is energetic, relational, and experiential. With the Gospel of Thomas (77), we can legitimately affirm, "Cleave the wood and I [the Christ] am there."

Whitehead notes that his vision of a lively, interactive, experiential universe reflects the insights of the nineteenth-century poets; it also describes the energetic world of today's quantum physicists and the sacramental world of the biblical and mystical traditions. Psalm 148 and 150 describe a world of praise in which every creature in its own unique way glorifies its Creator, honoring the divinity wisely moving through the universe and its own life:

> Praise the LORD!
> Praise the LORD from the heavens;
> > praise him in the heights!
> Praise him, all his angels;
> > praise him, all his host!
> Praise him, sun and moon;
> > > praise him, all you shining stars!
> > > Praise him, you highest heavens,
> > > and you waters above the heavens!
> Let them praise the name of the LORD,
> > for he commanded and they were created.
> He established them forever and ever;
> > he fixed their bounds, which cannot be passed.
> Praise the LORD from the earth,
> > you sea monsters and all deeps,
> fire and hail, snow and frost,
> > stormy wind fulfilling his command!
> Mountains and all hills,
> > fruit trees and all cedars!

---

13 Alfred North Whitehead, *Religion in the Making* (New York: World Publishing, 1972), 149.

Wild animals and all cattle,
    creeping things and flying birds!
Kings of the earth and all peoples,
    princes and all rulers of the earth!
Young men and women alike,
    old and young together!...
Let everything that breathes praise God!

Whitehead invites us to live in a world of praise, in which "God speaks to us everywhere" and "all nature sings and round me rings the music of the spheres."[14] Mysticism embeds us in God's creation and joins us with our human and non-human siblings.

Adventures of the Spirit. The lively, enchanted, and relational universe Whitehead imagines is also profoundly adventurous. Those who look backwards, fixated on past achievements and the enamored of the old-time religion are going against the grain of the universe and the creative advance of God. Within each moment of experience, possibilities lure us forward toward fulfillment in the present moment and its impact on the future. While many identify God solely as the source of order and law in the universe, God is equally concerned with novelty and evolution. We may praise God with the words "blessed assurance, Jesus is mine...this is my story this is my song, praising my savior all the day long."[15] but we would do well to assent to words attributed to William Sloan Coffin, "blessed disturber, I am his."

Mystical experience does not imprison us in the past or in an unchanging eternity, far from the maelstrom of history. Authentic spirituality plunges us into the dynamics of our experience and the energy of life which flows through us, aiming toward new and creative embodiments of God's vision. According to Whitehead,

> The worship of God is not a rule of safety – it is an adventure of spirit, the flight after the unattainable. The death

---

14 Maltbie Babcock, "This is my Father's World"
15 Fanny J. Crosby, "Blessed Assurance."

of religion comes with the repression of the high hope of adventure.[16]

Adventurous spirituality inspired Celtic monks to launch out into the Atlantic in rudderless coracles, trusting the winds of grace to lead them to their place of resurrection. Adventurous visions guided Sarah and Abraham, inspiring them to leave the familiar to venture toward their promised land. Adventurous images of freedom guided the steps of Harriet Tubman, Mahatma Gandhi, Nelson Mandela, and Martin Luther King. When we travel God's adventurous pathway, we can claim with Abraham Joshua Heschel, in reflecting on his experiences in the freedom marches in the South, "I felt like my legs were praying."

The Arc of the Universe Bends Toward Beauty. Whitehead's mystical vision is forward looking, inspiring a spiritual and ethical restlessness. The teleology of the universe, reflecting divine wisdom and creativity, is toward the emergence of beauty. Within each moment of experience, the future calls. God's vision for us is wholeness and intensity in this present moment, but also for the future. Just as Jesus grew in wisdom and stature, we are challenged to initiate novelty to match and go beyond the novelties of our environment. Mystics experience a sense of peace, grounded in self-transcendence and trust that their lives are treasured by God. But, within this peace, there is a creative and holy restlessness, an inner Divine Eros, flowing in and through them, aspiring toward abundant life for themselves and creation. The moral arc that aims toward wholeness flows through us toward the universe. This prophetic energy is both spiritual and moral and as it arcs it inspires us to be prophetic challengers of injustice and apathy. The adventures of ideas, reflective of the adventures of the spirit, call us beyond past spiritual and ethical achievements toward new horizons of love, embodied in persons and communities. In words Whitehead would affirm, cosmologically as well as politically, New England

16 Alfred North Whitehead, *Science and the Modern World* (New York: Free Press, 1997), 192.

pastor Theodore Parker captures the Eros of Universe aiming toward personal and planetary healing.

> Look at the facts of the world. You see a continual and progressive triumph of the right. I do not pretend to understand the moral universe, the arc is a long one, my eye reaches but little ways. I cannot calculate the curve and complete the figure by the experience of sight; I can divine it by conscience. But from what I see I am sure it bends towards justice.

Whitehead discerned a movement toward wholeness and novelty in the universe. The philosophical mystic is not content with the status quo. Implicated in the injustices of their time, mystics call their communities to move from self-interest to community-affirmation and eventually to world loyalty. Mystics are heavenly-minded, citizens of a realm that transcends personal ego and the present moment. They are also earthly good, challenging injustice inspired by their vision of what the world can be. Social activism and mysticism often walk hand in hand. The mystic's encounter with God inspires them to challenge anything, and most particularly institutional, economic, and governmental practices, that stand in the way of persons experiencing God's fullness in their lives.

Imitating God. At the heart of Whitehead's mystical vision is the quest for world consciousness. Though religious experience begins with solitude, our moments of solitude are inherently relational and inspire growth in wisdom and stature. Mystical experiences take us from self-interest and self-love to sacrificial love and world consciousness. Ever larger circles of spiritual experience take us from individual and filial loyalty to focus on community and nation and ultimately to world loyalty. Our calling is to become as like unto the divine as possible, as Plato counsels, recognizing that humans tend to become like the gods whom they worship. Coercive and authoritarian images of God lead to authoritarian doctrine-centered religions and coercive political policies. Relational and loving images of God lead to shared understandings of power and affirmation of diversity. In similar fashion, Whitehead describes the evolution of religious ritual and experience:

> A social consciousness concerns people whom you know and love individually. Hence, rightness is mixed up with the notion of preservation. Conduct is right which will lead some god to protect you; and it is wrong if it leads some being to compass your destruction. But a world-consciousness is more disengaged. It rises to the conception of the essential rightness of things... The new, and almost profane, concept of the goodness of God replaces the older emphasis on the will of God. In communal religion you study the will of God in order that he may preserve you; in a purified religion, rationalized under the influence of the world concept, you study his goodness in order to be like him. It is the difference between the enemy you conciliate and the companion you imitate.[17]

To recapitulate, small visions of God lead to constricted ethical, political, and religious experiences, ruled by fear rather than love, and separating the world into saved and unsaved, friend and foe, and elect and reprobate. Large visions of God embrace the world in its complexity and tragic beauty. Whiteheads envisions God as cosmic, as the Infinite-Intimate, whose creative-responsive love inspires each moment of experience and the evolutionary process and embraces the universe in its totality. God is in all things, and all things are in God. Ruling by love, "God is the poet of the world with tender patience leading it by his vision of truth, beauty, and goodness."[18]

God is the universal and ultimate model of relationship, adventure, experience, and artistry. God is our companion, guiding each moment of experience with an array of possibilities for intensity and fullness of experience for itself and the world beyond. God is the source of adventure, inspiring our own adventures and

---

17 Alfred North Whitehead, *Religion in the Making* (New York: World Publishing, 1972), 39-40.

18 Alfred North Whitehead, *Process and Reality: Corrected Edition*, 346.

the ground of novelty, luring us to innovative spiritual and ethical experiences.

As the reality "in whom we live and move and have our being," (Acts 17:28), God is readily available to all creation. The sighs too deep for words in our hearts and minds reflect the deeper groanings of creation. Experiencing God is not a voyage from the alone to the Alone, as Plotinus counsels, but an invitation to join solitude and community as two essential components of relational spirituality. Because God is all-inclusive, the counsel to "be perfect as God is perfect" challenges us to embrace as much of reality as possible, recognizing that all things to greater or lesser degree, reflect divine artistry and inspiration.

Peace that Passes Personality. The quest for wholeness of experience lures us to wider and wider circles of ethics and spirituality. As Nicholas of Cusa and Bonaventure assert, God is a sphere, or circle, whose center is everywhere and whose circumference is nowhere. God centers and inspires each of us and all creation. Divine possibilities are mediated to us through every encounter. In the language of mystics, God is revealed to us in every face. We are, accordingly, kin to all things. From this perspective, the peace that passes all understanding, does not anesthetize us to the pain of the world, but joins our experience with that of the "fellow sufferer who understands."[19] In synch with God's vision, we become mahatmas, bodhisattvas, and little Christs, whose spirits reach to the stars and descend to the cellular. We become people of peace, sharing in God's experience of tragic beauty, looking beyond our self-interest, and fulfilling our vocation as God's companions in healing the world.

> Peace is the quality of mind steady in its reliance that fine action is treasured in the nature of things....Peace is self-control at its widest – at the width where the 'self' has been lost

---

19 Alfred North Whitehead, *Process and Reality*, 351.

and interest has been transferred to coordinations beyond personality.[20]

World loyalty and commitment to love others as oneself widen the self, enabling us to share in everlasting life in a world of constant change. While mystics may be prophets, restless in their quest for justice, their restlessness is tempered by knowledge that they are companions with God in healing the earth and its people. Such vision energizes and inspires and calms.

Concluding Words. While Alfred North Whitehead never described himself as a mystic, he invokes the significance of mysticism and heightened consciousness in the formation of philosophy and theology. Whitehead's metaphysical vision is holistic and mystical, emerging from the interplay of analysis, intuition, reflection, and breadth of thought. Whitehead presents a metaphysical mysticism, not unlike philosophers such as Plato, Plotinus, Nicolas of Cusa, and William James. Whitehead's mysticism is grounded in the vision of a dynamic God-filled universe, in which God is the inspiration of novelty, restlessness, and creativity. Whiteheadian mysticism inspires us to plunge into the every-flowing stream of life, embracing relatedness and claiming our role as God's companions in healing the earth. Though a theoretician, Whitehead's vision was grounded in experience and provides pathways to experience the process-relational vision in daily life. Like the philosopher Whitehead, we need to take time to observe the totality of our experience, explore alternative visions, and put them in practice as companions in promoting novel visions and behaviors to respond to the novelties of our time.

Whitehead's philosophical mysticism gave birth to process-relational theology. Concrete in orientation, process-relational theology embeds us in the world of change, inspiring us to be agents in transforming the world, companioning with God in healing the earth.

---

20   Alfred North Whitehead, *Adventures of Ideas* (New York: Free Press, 1969), 274, 285.

Chapter Three

On the Road With Whitehead

The process is the reality and the reality is the process. Movement energizes and expands our theological and philosophical visions. While doctrine stands still, rooted in one place and inflexible, freezing revelation in abstract concepts and rules, process moves forward, transformed by spiritual experiences and encounters with other spiritual seekers. Inspired by the flow of the universe, process-relational theology is an adventure of ideas, issuing in life-transforming behaviors.

Walking with Whitehead inspires us to join theology, spirituality, and ethics. It is an adventure in what I have described as "theo-spirituality," the intimate connectedness of theological reflection, spiritual experience, and ethical and social activism, challenging us to move from self-interest to world loyalty, and individual to planetary consciousness.

The meanderings of this book describe a month of meditations, joining theological reflection inspired by Whitehead's writings with issues of twenty-first century spirituality and ethics. My walks took me from the cosmos to seashells on the beach, from sea breezes to breaking news, from prayer to protest, from idealism to pragmatic progressivism. Rooted in the movement of our times, this text was written with a cosmic vision as well as the backdrop of a hard-fought USA presidential election, presidential prevarication about the election results, Black Lives Matter and change protests, domestic terrorists storming the USA Capitol, a global pandemic in which scientists were seen as both heroes and traitors, and the public surfacing of Christian nationalism and the conflation of political figures with God's will. In the quiet of Cape Cod beaches and my home study, I sought to be both heavenly minded and earthly good and to live in the spirit of the Hebraic prophets who joined profound insight into God's ways with protesting in justice in the quest for Shalom.

I invite you to read this text meditatively at whatever pace you deem best for your theological and spiritual growth. You may take time to reflect on the passage with which each chapter begins, enjoy a walk opening to insights from the passage, and then read my reflections. Process-relational theology encourages creativity. Whitehead's and my words are the beginning of the journey, an invitation to experience process theology in your own way.

George Bernard Shaw once suggested that the professions are conspiracies against the laity. Accordingly, I privilege lay insights as much as academic expertise. The adventure of ideas is the gift of imagination, innovation, inspiration, and integrity, not adherence to inflexible scholasticism.

Take time to meditate on these passages. Become a "theo-spiritual" theologian yourself. Be the mystic only you can be. Let these contemplations stir new inspirations and inspire actions to heal the world.

A Month of Meditations for Process-Relational Pilgrims

1.

Adventurous Spirituality

> *The worship of God is not a rule of safety – it is an adventure of the spirit. A flight after the unattainable. The death of religion comes with the repression of the high hope of adventure.*[21]

In C.S. Lewis' *The Lion, The Witch, and the Wardrobe,* Susan, one of the future queens of Narnia, enquires about the Great Lion King, Aslan, "Is he – safe?" Mr. Beaver responds, "Safe? Who said anything about safe? 'Course he isn't safe. But he's good. He's the King, I tell you."

Many persons are surprised at reading Whitehead's description of worship as unsafe. We identify religion with greater peace of mind, comfort, and calm. We take solace in the "old time religion" in times of personal and social change. We need comfort when our world is turned upside down. For many, religion is the last bastion of the status quo, untouched by science, technology, globalism, race, and sexuality. To such believers, scriptural witness is unchanging, and so is God who is the ultimate justification for clinging to the past. We go to church, they believe, to escape the hardscrabble world of politics, economics, and social change. Whitehead recognizes the importance of order and changelessness, and even speaks of God as the principle of limitation and ground of order. Yet, God is also the organ of novelty, and the universe constantly joins order and novelty, and predictability and surprise, in its ongoing evolution. In that spirit, American author Annie Dillard advises people to strap themselves to their pews and wear crash helmets to church just in case the Holy Spirit shows up and shakes everything up as She did on Pentecost. Whitehead recognizes that authentic worship of a multi-billion galaxy, constantly evolving God, can threaten our

---

21   Alfred North Whitehead, *Science and the Modern World* (New York: Free Press, 1967), 192. The Lowell Lectures, 1925.

certainties and turn our world upside down. Worship can challenge the comfortable, as well as comfort the troubled.

Whitehead cites the words of a hymn, "Abide with me/fast falls the eventide," as definitive of the nature of things, spiritually and cosmologically. The "Dude Abides," so says Jeffrey "the Dude," Lebowski, in the film, "The Great Lebowski." We need realities that abide whether in terms of long-term and faithful relationships, institutions we can trust, the predictability of the seasons, and stability on our small and "swiftly tilting planet." Yet, the evening falls quickly. Life is, as Whitehead asserts, perpetually perishing. The immediacy of the present dies giving birth to the next moment of experience. Shift happens, rocking our world!

The author of Lamentations 3, writing in a time of national upheaval, reminds his readers:

> The steadfast love of the LORD never ceases,
>> his mercies never come to an end;
> they are new every morning;
>> great is your faithfulness. (Lamentations 3:22-23)

These words touched my spirit, providing both comfort and challenge, as I watched from the safety of my home the terrorist attack on the USA Capitol on January 6, 2021. I needed to find something secure in a world turned upside down. I also needed inspiration to respond wisely to the rising tide of white and Christian nationalism.

God is faithful and God is constantly doing a new thing. God is steadfast just as God is definitively ever-creative and transformational. Reflecting God's nature, the eighth and seventh century BCE prophets of Israel embody the restlessness of creative transformation and social critique. They present a jarring and unsettling contrast to institutional injustice and idolatry of their time – and ours. The prophetic word is always unsafe to those who want to hold onto life as it has been and who fear that change will threaten their privilege. The prophets not only reflect God's ongoing critique of unjust social structures but also God's dynamic, evolving, and innovative vision of history guided by God's vision of Shalom.

Religion without adventure is dead! That's a strong statement. But can you imagine the sea without waves? Can you imagine air without wind? Can you think of a heart not beating? Can you visualize yourself frozen in the same spot, physically, spiritually, or intellectually? Long before the death of God movement of the 1960's or John Shelby Spong, Whitehead saw unchanging faith as dying faith.

Adventure is at the heart of reality and humankind's spiritual sojourn. Gautama leaves palatial opulence in quest for enlightenment. Isaiah is confronted by the God of the universe while seeking a quiet place for prayer in a time of national upheaval. Ruth must journey from the familiarity of her Moabite home to companion her mother-in-law Naomi as an immigrant to Bethlehem, and then become the "good ancestor" of King David and Jesus of Nazareth. Queen Esther must put her life at risk to save her people from genocide for "just such a time as this." Saul, soon to be Paul, must give up the structures of his childhood faith to embrace God's message of grace in Jesus of Nazareth.

Whitehead believes that the spiritual adventures of humankind reflect and provide evidence for the universe's deeper cosmic and microcosmic journeys. In a world of arising and perishing galaxies and solar systems, there is no ultimate safety, if you define safety in terms of clinging to that which does not change. Our lives moment by moment are unsafe as we confront new experiences and encounter new demands, even those that are built into the nature of physical, emotional, and spiritual maturation. Learning to walk demands courage of a toddler. The first day of school can produce anxiety and insecurity for parent and child alike. Adolescence and falling in love are confusing. Aging, as the adage goes, is not for sissies. Then there is the final adventure of death and dying, frightening yet promising, all at the same time.

Transformation is built into the nature of things. The pure conservative, whether in science, culture, or religion, Whitehead avers, goes against the nature of the universe. Backward looking faith turns its back on God's new creation. Stifling adventure destroys persons, nations, and planets. Stifling adventure destroys faith.

Spirituality embraces, albeit at times uncomfortably, the precarious nature of life and the fallibility of our institutions. Spirituality, to use a Whiteheadian comment, embraces novelty in response to the novelty of the world. Spirituality, as response to divinity, invites us to align ourselves with the One who is both faithful and challenging, who brings order to the universe and provokes personal and social transformation.

An Unsafe Practice. To embrace the interplay of order and novelty, take time to reread imaginatively the passage from Lamentations:

> The steadfast love of the LORD never ceases,
>   his mercies never come to an end;
>   they are new every morning;
>   great is your faithfulness. (3:22-23)

Visualize moments of stability and order in your life. Upon what realities do you depend. Where have you found wholeness through stability and structure?

Visualize moments of creative transformation and change. Visualize times when change was thrust upon you. Imagine moments when life called you to take a new path of life, to risk the familiar and comfortable to be faithful to the future beckoning God. Where have you encountered God as unsafe in terms of your personal, relational, or professional status quo? Where do you see "unsafe" life-supporting changes emerging from God's presence in our culture and institutional life? What must we risk to be in alignment with the moral and spiritual arc of the universe? Give thanks to the God of change and glory, the God of adventure and companionship.

2.

Religion will not regain its old power until it can face change in the same spirit as does science. Its principles may be eternal, but the expression of these principles requires continual development…A clash of doctrines is not a disaster, it is an opportunity.[22]

Over the past two years (2020-2022), we have lived through a time of pandemic. During this unprecedented time, many people have come to understand more clearly the nature of scientific exploration. They have discovered that scientific knowledge is always evolving and never final in the quest for truth and healing. We have learned much about the spread, prevention, treatment, and vaccination process related to COVID 19, a word most of us had never heard before late January 2020. Our science has evolved, correcting errors, adding to the body of knowledge and practical application, and will continue to evolve as we learn more about the pandemic and its impact on our physical, emotional, and spiritual health.

To some persons during this time of pandemic the evolution of scientific knowledge has been frustrating and a source of skepticism. Not understanding the nature of scientific exploration, these scientific naysayers and COVID deniers have seen science in terms of unchanging absolutes. Any changes or corrections of previous knowledge provide reason for doubt and disregard of any scientific information. If Dr. Anthony Fauci rethinks an earlier prediction, they assume his current correction discredits his current position regarding contagion and treatment.

In contrast to the belief that scientific statements are absolute and unchanging, the scientific adventure is always in process, expanding, correcting, sometimes meandering on the way to deeper understandings of our personal lives and the universe, whether it relates to the pandemic or the age of the planet. Doubt is not the admission of defeat but the path to greater clarity and truth. Scientific dead ends may be detours to new vistas of understanding.

---

22   Whitehead, *Science and the Modern World,* 189, 186.

When I was growing up in the 1950's, most of us imagined that there was only one galaxy, the Milky Way. In six decades since my childhood, we have expanded our galactic census from a billion to forty billion to now a trillion galaxies, acknowledging that "trillion" is shorthand for "more than we can count or imagine."

Like science, healthy religion is exploratory and evolving in nature. Religion begins with experiencing the Holy, whether in a sky full of stars, a voice in a burning bush, a bright light on the road to Damascus, inner voice of conscience, a strangely warmed heart, or a prophetic challenge. These encounters with the Holy are always concrete, timebound, and historical. Revelation requires a receiver, and the receiver experiences revelation from their personal and cultural perspective. While we cannot separate doctrine from experience, doctrines emerge as ways of understanding, clarifying, and sharing our community's unique and foundational experiences of the Holy. Our theological reflections and doctrinal statements are important in our spiritual formation and shape our understanding of future revelations as well as promote experiences of the Holy. Still, our doctrines and theological statements are finite and subject to transformation as we have further encounters with the Holy and new experiences of challenge and contrast. As the apostle Paul asserts, "we have this treasure in clay jars, so that it may be made clear that this extraordinary power belongs to God and does not come from us." (2 Corinthians 4:7)

In 1955, just three years after my birth, Will Herberg wrote *Protestant, Catholic, Jew* to describe the contours of North American religion. In my hometown in the Salinas Valley, California, these were the only religious options available. But, by my junior year in high school, I began a spiritual quest that included American Transcendentalism (Emerson and Thoreau), Hinduism, and Buddhism. My youthful spiritual quest, eventuating in learning Transcendental Meditation at an ashram in Berkeley, California, as a first-year college student, reflected the growing impact of global spiritualities on North American religious life. Encounters with other religious traditions, not unlike encounters with biology, evolutionary theory, physics, and cosmology, deepen our understanding of God and reshape our religious visions. Religions grow in their encounters with contrasting and complementary spiritual experiences and practices.

In the face of religious pluralism, some Christians cling to absolutes, believing that any alternations in the "old-time religion" threaten the existence of faith itself. Accordingly, they hold onto images of six-day creation, young earth, and human uniqueness, despite scientific evidence of a grand and evolving universe from which humankind emerges. As these Christians encounter other faiths, they built similar bulwarks against change and growth, dividing the world into truth and error, and saved and unsaved. They assume that any embrace of change, any questioning of their version of scriptural or institutional infallibility or the complexities of human life, puts the entire edifice of faith at risk.

Process-relational theology affirms, with Alfred North Whitehead, that the phrase "religion in the making" applies to every living religion tradition. This statement is true not only in the origins and emergence of religious traditions but in evolution of religious traditions today. Faith traditions are alive and lively, constantly growing and changing in light new experiences, whether scientific, cosmological, or spiritual. Process-relational theologies see contrasts and challenges as opportunities for reflection. All religion is relative and subject to creative transformation. As we train our eyes on the far horizons of moral and spiritual arcs of history, we discover there is always greater light to be shed on our scriptures, practices, and theologies.

Healthy religion promotes ongoing reflection and reformation. Lively religion encourages its followers to grow in wisdom and stature. Contrasts are an opportunity to explore new paths of spirituality. Accordingly, the current phenomenon of inter-spirituality is congruent with faithfulness to God. We can grow in faith by joining Transcendental Meditation with Centering Prayer, Lectio Divina with Zen Meditation, and Genesis 1 with 21st Century cosmology. What appears to be a clash can be an invitation to holy adventure in walking the paths of God.

A Developing Spiritual Practice. Begin with a few moments of silence, quietly listening to the flow of thoughts, emotions, and bodily responses. Listen in stillness to the wonder of this simple moment, being alive and active. In a time of personal self-examination, consider your spiritual, intellectual, and ethical growth over the course of your life from childhood to the present day. What certainties have you left behind? What past experiences still shape your life? What new routes have you taken spiritually, religiously, and personally? As you look at your life, what changes do you imagine occurring in the near and far future? What changes in terms of personal life, relationships, faith, and activity do you envision? How do you feel about letting go of your current familiarities?

As you ponder the currents of change flowing through your life and drawing you forward, where do you imagine God on the journey ahead? How do you imagine God's nature as a fellow pilgrim? In what ways might you stay in touch with God through the changes of life? Abraham and Sarah built altars as they moved forward by stages from Haran to the promised land. What "altars" might you erect to experience God on the journey ahead?

3.

Religion is the vision of something that stands beyond, be-hind, and within the passing flux of immediate things; something which is real, and yet waiting to be realized; something which is a remote possibility, and yet the greatest of present facts; something that gives meaning to all that passes, and yet eludes apprehen-sion; something whose possession is the final good, and yet beyond all reach; something which is the ultimate ideal and the hopeless quest.[23]

When I was a child, one of my favorite programs was "One Step Beyond." A precursor to the "Twilight Zone," this weekly program, hosted by John Nuland, told stories about persons who unexpectedly journeyed beyond everyday experience into the para-normal. They discovered that the daily dimensions of consciousness were just the tip of the iceberg. The characters in the drama real-ized, to their amazement and terror, and occasional solace, that heights and depths of reality are hidden from us, until till we take a step beyond "normalcy" into past lives, premonitions, and thin places where time and eternity meet. That step beyond everyday reality may fill us with amazement, awe, and fear and trembling, and it may also imbue everyday life with a sense of holiness and every day with the vision of a holy adventure. Indeed, what we perceive as "normal" may hide the deeper dimensions of life. Like the children of *The Lion, The Witch, and The Wardrobe*, we may discover a doorway into an enchanted reality with dimensions and possibilities beyond what we had previously imagined in the most unlikely place – a wardrobe in an unused room. We may discover that while we are children, or non-descript people on earth, we are kings and queens, people of great stature, in Narnia.

Whitehead recognized that consciousness was the tip of the experiential iceberg. Everyday consciousness is grounded in a vast sea of causal relationships of which we are typically unaware. With-in those unconscious relationships, we experience the heaviness

---

23 Whitehead, *Science and the Modern World*, 191-192.

of the past, the firing of synapses, shadowy collective memories of our human and non-human ancestors, the depths from which dreams emerge, and a sense of the interplay of permanence and flux within which the present moment finds its home. We come to realize that the whole universe conspires to create each moment of experience. What happens on a distant galaxy touches us, the movements of the stars shape our emotional lives and give birth to astrological ruminations, past repressed trauma and grief may limit and sensitize us to the pain of others, and the ambient sense of trust emerging from positive parenting gives birth to optimism and initiative. These hidden experiences unite the heights and depths of life. The presence of God in the place of "sighs too deep for words" bursts forth in mystical experiences, synchronicities, intuitions, and life-changing healing energy. The mountaintop of revelatory moments gives perspective which guides our daily commitments.

Whitehead asserts that religious traditions arise from these extraordinary mystical experiences which, despite their uniqueness, are believed to reveal the deepest dimensions of reality and the goals of human life. According to the philosopher, "Religion claims that its concepts, though derived primarily from special experiences, are yet of universal validity, to be applied by faith to the ordering of all experience."[24] There is no religion without mysticism, whether it be Moses confronted by a voice from the burning bush, Jacob dreaming of a ladder of angels and later wrestling with a nocturnal deity, Isaiah encountering the God of the universe in the Jerusalem Temple, Buddha meditating under the Bo Tree, Mohammed hearing God's voice in a cave, or Jesus appearing to Mary of Magdala in the Garden of Gethsemane and to his disciples in an upper room on Easter night, breathing on them and energizing and orienting their spiritual journeys.

Whitehead recognizes that the *kataphatic and apophatic* – with images and beyond images – describe our experience of God's presence in the world. The *kataphatic* proclaims the immanence and

---

24 Alfred North Whitehead, *Religion in the Making* (New York: Macmillan, 1926), 31.

intimacy of God, and points to the personal origins of the universe in God's creative and loving wisdom. God is embedded in the world. Divinity is embodied in each moment of life through aims and visions that give birth and guide our personal and corporate adventures. The whole world is an incarnation of God. The Word and Wisdom of God takes residence in a humble manger and is witnessed in every newborn's face.

In contrast to the aesthetic and ethical immanence of *kataphatic* spirituality, *apophatic* spirituality points to the transcendence, infinity, and indescribability of God. No creature fully expresses God's vision. If you say you know it, it is not God, avers Augustine of Hippo. "Neti, Neti," cries the Hindu sage. "God is not this, not that." All creatures, including humans, experience God but always in terms of our limitations and perspectives. Dogs experience God in terms of canine experience, rejoicing in sprinting on a Cape Cod beach and nuzzling against their human companions. Pangolins experience God looking downward as they quest for insects. Right whales rejoice in God breaching off Nantucket Sound. Humans experience God in terms of our concrete human nervous system, religious movements, cultural and scientific achievements, past experiences, and the concrete limitations and possibilities of human life. God is here, and God is more. The apophatic approach, spirituality without images, reminds us that God is always more than we can imagine. No word fully describes God. Our theologies are, as Zen Buddhists proclaim, fingers pointing toward the moon and not the moon itself.

The whole earth is full of God's glory, the angels chant in praise in the Jerusalem Temple, and Isaiah is transformed. The world is aflame with divine grandeur, and we are transfigured. We glimpse God's vision through our spiritual practices. Prayer, meditation, and mission align us with God's vision of Shalom and inspire us to be God's companions in healing the world. Still, the moral and spiritual arc lure us toward the far horizon beyond our current experience.

Our quests from God remind us that Divinity is "the ideal and the hopeless quest." Still, it is the quest that transforms our lives and provides a polestar for the quest for justice and Shalom. Theodore Parker captures the "impossible dream" of justice-seeking that motivated his quest to abolish slavery in the United States. "Look at the facts of the world. You see a continual and progressive triumph of the right. I do not pretend to understand the moral universe, the arc is a long one, my eye reaches but little ways. I cannot calculate the curve and complete the figure by the experience of sight; I can divine it by conscience. But from what I see I am sure it bends towards justice."

We need the far horizon. We need alternative visions, not yet born and beyond our current reach, to inspire our justice seeking and peacemaking. Whitehead once said that "It is more important that a proposition be interesting than that it be true. This statement is almost a tautology. For the energy of a counterfactual or imaginative proposition in an occasion of experience is its interest and is its importance its lure to new dimensions. But, of course, a true proposition, connected though not limited by our factual realities, is more apt to be interesting than a false one."[25] The counterfactual, the creative alternative, the impossible dream, the unrealized hope, the interesting proposition, lure us forward to open horizons, and toward the dream that these "interesting propositions" might take shape in the actualities of experience.

Reality is more than "we can ask or imagine." God is more than we can ever conceive. The Spirit restlessly cries out for more – for the experience of more light, love, and liberty. Hope is the unseen passion that draws us toward a "more perfect union." Our current doctrines and rituals point beyond themselves to deeper dimensions of life. These theological guideposts and places of spiritual nourishment point us beyond themselves to that place from which dreams are made, the Shalom vision of the lion with the lamb, swords into plowshares, victorious love, and laughter of children in every street and hamlet.

---

25 *Adventures in Ideas*, 244.

A Visionary Practice. Taking seriously Whitehead's connection of spirituality with solitude (see affirmation #4), draw away from the crowd for a time of reflection – perhaps, through contemplative prayer, visualizing possibilities, leaving home for a walk in a quiet place. As you spiritually saunter, let your mind wander, let your thoughts graze beyond your "normal" life. Prayerfully roam into possibilities that are real but not actually present. What "impossibilities" lure you forward? What dreams energize you? What "hopeless" ideals motivate you to new adventures?

The great adventures of life often involve a sense of impossibility, an idealism beyond the "realism" of everyday life. A breaking down of roadblocks to new dimensions. Imaginative ideals, hopeless impossibilities, and adventures of ideas plant the seeds of the better world to come, the larger self to explore and share with others.

4.

Religion is what an individual does with his solitariness…
if you are never solitary, you are never religious.[26]

This morning I set out before sunrise on a hike to the tip of Long Beach here in Centerville. For over an hour, on the first day of 2021, I was truly alone. No fellow walkers with whom to exchange greetings. No pop tunes or talk radio blaring from a parking lot car. Just the sounds of the waves lapping and an occasion sea gull or piping plover. Solitude to let the universe flow in and through me. Quiet to hear my inner voices and an unplanned insight. Solitude to live in the moment on this thin stretch of seashore and yet feel the grandeur of infinite space-time. Yet in solitude I feel the call of the world of pandemic and protest, not as a source of anger or anxiety, but compassionate companionship.

Alfred North Whitehead is perhaps the most relational philosopher in the Western philosophical tradition. Whitehead preaches that relationship defines reality and is foundational to process-relational ethics. The whole universe conspires to create each moment of experience and each moment of experience shapes the future beyond itself. Reality is, as process philosopher Charles Hartshorne asserts, is a "social process." Even God is caught up in the fabric of relatedness. God touches each moment of experience with ideals, or initial aims, relevant to its environment. God also experiences every moment of experience letting it shape God's experience. God is the fellow sufferer who understands and the intimate companion who celebrates.

Solitude and relationship are polarities defining reality and the human adventure. Each moment emerges from its environment and enjoys the privacy of self-creation. Relationship requires solitude in human life and in the cosmic adventure. After a day of healing and teaching relationships, Jesus rises the next morning to go to a solitary place to pray and discern the next steps of his

---

26 Alfred North Whitehead, *Religion in the Making* (New York: Macmillan, 1926).

ministry. Gautama's forty years of public teaching are grounded in years of contemplation and his enlightenment experience under the Bo Tree. Queen Esther retreats for a time of prayer to discern how she should respond to the threat of genocide in "just such a time as this."

Far from the maelstrom of cable news, online news flashes, and relational and work demands, solitude enables us to reflect on our experiences and draw away from group think. Solitude frees us from social and religious norms and unassailable doctrines and cultural mores. To find relational and spiritual wholeness, there must be "spaces in our togetherness," as poet Kahlil Gibran avers. Ironically, deep contemplation gives us wider perspectives on the world in which we live. In silencing the many voices of our companions and the culture around us, we discern the "sighs too deep for words" emerging from the movements of God's Spirit in our spirit. We feel the universe flowing through us, moving though our individual experience to the far reaches of the cosmos.

Whitehead believes that each moment of experience emerges from the influence of God's initial aim, or unique vision, for that moment and its environment. God is moving amid the many influences that shape each moment, providing an ideal, nudge, insight, sense of calm order, and creative restlessness. Most of the time, we are unaware of God's vision for any given moment as it emerges from the unconscious to conscious experience. We have agendas of our own and are often blown about by the demands of the moment. In silence, we pause and notice. We listen to our lives and hear the deeper voice of God in symphony with our own deeper yearnings. Simply present to the moment we feel the pulse of divine possibility birthing and guiding the Holy Here and Now.

Amid a time of national crisis, the author of Psalm 46 counsels, "be still and know that I am God." An alternative translation is "pause awhile and know that I am God." In the silence of his bed, we like Samuel call out to God, "Speak, your servant is listening." Seeking refuge from an angry potentate, Elijah stands on the mountain watching the storm pass by, only to experience God in a still, small voice.

Each moment brings divine messages. As a popular slogan of the United Church of Christ affirms, "God is still speaking," provoking the insightful and ironic response, "Is anyone listening?"

God's aim typically comes without herald, blending in with the totality of our experience. There is, as Whitehead states, no independent religious sense distinct from our typical patterns of experiencing the world. Religious experiences emerge within everyday experiences of action and contemplation. Even profoundly mystical experiences arise through the normal, albeit deeper, causal relationships that characterize emotion, imagination, and sense experience. In solitude, we see more clearly and deeply, if we dedicate our solitariness to divine inspiration.

We can discern God in communal worship and among crowds. Many of us have experienced a greater sense of God's purpose in reaching out to vulnerable persons. Acts of kindness deepen our spirits and widen our world. Travel presents us with novel experiences of human diversity and awakens us to the gifts of other cultures. The Trappist Monk and spiritual guide Thomas Merton describes discovering God's presence as he walked the streets of Louisville, Kentucky: "At the corner of Fourth and Walnut, in the center of the shopping district, I was suddenly overwhelmed with the realization that I loved all those people, that they were mine and I was theirs, that we could not be alien to one another even though we were total strangers. It was like waking from a dream of separateness...The whole illusion of separate holy existence is a dream." Still, Merton's embrace of community was inspired by hours of contemplative prayer. Alone with his thoughts that day in Louisville, Merton felt the pulse of life flow through him, connecting him with humanity in its wondrous diversity.

Like Martin Luther King, Merton discovered that we can picket and pray. Mystical empathy in concert with God leads to empathy with the joys and sorrows of all creation. Postponing enlightenment after decades of meditation, the Bodhisattva's spiritual equanimity inspires kinship with creation until every creature finds peace of mind.

In silence, we discover that every intuition and encounter can be an epiphany. Springing from the inner journey, our outer adventures shimmer with the energy of love. Listening to our lives, we let our lives speak in acts of loving kindness intended to heal the world.

In Search of the Nearest Faraway Place.[27] Solitude is a moment away. Each moment's self-creation is solitary even in a crowd. There is a depth in each of us that no one, including ourselves, can fully fathom. The divine energy, what Whitehead calls the initial aim, joins eternity and temporality, and infinity and finitude. Opening to this divine energy of love, from which all worlds emerge, can happen unbidden in a flash, but most of us need to spiritual practices to cleanse the doors of perception.

Is there a sacred place in your life? To me, it is the Craigville Beaches where I roamed daily, hail, snow, and bracing wind, in the writing of this book. It is also my "arts and crafts" reclining chair where I write, study, and meditate daily. When we lived in a Chevy Chase, Maryland, high rise in 2012-2013, I found an acre glade a few blocks from home where my young grandson and I would play and imbibe on the insights of a two year old and his sixty year old grandparent. Our perambulations and peripatetic conversations gave birth to two books, *The Gospel According to Winnie the Pooh* and *Piglet's Process: Process Theology for All God's Children.*

There is a nearest faraway place within you and all around you. Take some time to embrace the still, small voice of divine possibility and energy in your "thin place," where time and eternity meet.

---

27 Inspired by an instrumental by the Beach Boys, composed by Bruce Johnston.

5.

*In communal religion you study the will of God in order that
[God] may preserve you; in a purified, rational religion, rational-
ized under the influence of the world concept, you study [God's]
goodness in order to be like [God]. It is the difference between the
enemy you conciliate and the companion you imitate.*[28]

Process theologian and Bible scholar Terence Fretheim says
that while most people think "do you believe in God?" is the central religious question, a more important question is "what kind
of God do you believe in?" What is the character of the God you
worship? What is God's relationship to the world? What is God's
relationship to suffering and evil? Is God out to hurt us or heal us?
Is God best experienced in terms of love or power?

Whitehead describes the evolution of religion from tribal to
global, parochial to global, and punitive to graceful. Although
Whitehead recognizes unique mystical experiences and theological
affirmations that promote world loyalty, he also realizes that "com
munal" or "tribal" religion is often the norm in religious experience.
Often God is described as punitive, vengeful, violent, and divisive.
Authoritarian visions of God inspire authoritarian religious and political structures. Binary understandings of God separate the world
into saved and unsaved, and elect and damned, and may lead to
privileging the saved ethically and politically and neglecting – and
ostracizing – the unsaved. If God has abandoned certain segments
of the population, these segments of the population, whether based
on sexuality, national of origin, or religious affiliation, do not deserve our ethical consideration. The rise of Christian nationalism in
the United States, similar in form to Muslim or Hindu nationalism
and extremism, joins God and politics seamlessly, separating the
world into friend and foe, denying any virtue or validity to those
whose opinions or lifestyle they determine as heretical or immoral.
Such binary, violent understandings of God lead to terrorists flying

---

28 Ibid., 40.

into the Twin Towers and taking to their knees in prayer before storming the USA Capitol with murder on their minds!

Authoritarian, binary, and fundamentalist religions would do well to remember Reinhold Niebuhr's counsel: we need to recognize the truth in our neighbor's falsehood and the falsehood in our own truth. Humility as well as generality is the salt of religion. Our most deeply-help doctrines and religious practices are finite, imperfect, perspectival, and open to revision. God is God and we are not. God is ultimate. In contrast, all our viewpoints are evolving and at best penultimate. We see, as the Apostle Paul observes, into a mirror dimly, at best knowing only partially. Letting God be God and being ourselves as humans, seeking to be fully human and fully blessed, in all our wondrous imperfection.

Rational or global religion reflects universalist visions of God. God's way with the world is inclusive, welcoming, and affirmative. God is, as Nicholas of Cusa and Bonaventure affirm, a sphere, or circle, whose center is everywhere and whose circumference is nowhere. All creation is centered in God. You are at the center of God's love. And so is everyone else! God's love embraces all creation. There is no outside to grace, compassion, or salvation.

While some imitate a bloodthirsty, judgmental, binary God, Whitehead's God, inspiring and embracing all creation, invites us to be all-inclusive in our love. Beloved by God, we see all creation as kin. While conflict and contrast are realities we must face personally, politically, and in the scrum of national security, we see holiness, not the demonic, in those whom we must confront ethically, politically, militarily, or in the justice system. We must fight injustice, but also see the presence in God in those who see themselves as our opponents. Alfred North Whitehead, Howard Thurman, Martin Luther King, Dorothy Day, Cesar Chavez, Oscar Romero, and Delores Huerta reveal the spirit of "prophetic healing," the intersection of prophetic confrontation and compassion. "Be perfect as God is," embodying God's compassion and empathy, and God's inclusion and creativity, as your joyful response to God's companioning love.

An Exercise in Imitating God. The Pre-Socratic philosopher Xenophanes (570-478 BCE) stated that if horses had gods, they would depict them like horses. While I believe that our most noble images of God come ultimately come from inspirational, mystical, and ethical experiences, we cannot avoid injecting our human biases and limitations. We are always tempted to create a God in our image, whether as male, authoritarian, violent, and domineering, or as beyond gender, loving, compassionate, and relational. I believe the great faiths at their best see God in terms of loving power and creative wisdom. Still, we need to examine our images of God and the images held by our religious and political leaders and their followers.

In a period of spiritual examination, prayerfully reflect on the following questions: How has your image of God evolved since childhood? How do you currently view God – personal, impersonal, intimate, distant?

In the stillness, ask God to reveal a deeper insight into God's presence in your life. In the day ahead, be attentive to divine inspirations coming in insights, intuitions, inspirations, and encounters, giving thanks for being a sounding board of divine revelation.

6.

Generality is the salt of religion.[29]

As a child, I recall seeing New Testament scholar and transla-
tor J.B. Phillip's book, *Your God is too Small* on a bookshelf in my
father's study. Phillips called on believers and seekers to reflect on
their images of God and assess whether they speak to their 20th
century experience. Our images of God always point to something
beyond our imaginations and are always in need of ongoing reformation and recreation. Even atheists have images of God. When a
professed atheist engages me in conversation, I don't usually seek
to persuade them to believe in the existence of God. I ask them,
"Tell me about the God you don't believe in." Often, we discover
that if God were like the atheist describes, neither one of us would
claim to be believers!

The phrase "go big or go home" has entered the public lex-
icon over the past few decades to challenge people and political
leaders to think big, act extravagantly, and challenge self-imposed
limitations. "Go big or go home" also applies to the evolution of
spiritual traditions and the tension between small and large, and
exclusive and inclusive, visions of God's existence and the human
adventure. Process-relational theologian Bernard Loomer sees "size"
or "stature" at the heart of the spiritual quest. Jesus grew in wisdom
and stature and understanding of God's vision for his life, as the
Temptations in the wilderness suggest, and that is our calling – and
our spiritual and political calling - as well. According to Loomer,
in a passage I invoked earlier, one that should be a mantra for process-relational spirituality:

> By size I mean the stature of a person's soul, the range
> and depth of his love, his capacity for relationships. I mean the
> volume of life you can take into your being and still maintain
> your integrity and individuality, the intensity and variety of
> outlook you can entertain in the unity of your being without

---

29 Ibid., 42.

feeling defensive or insecure. I mean the strength of your spirit to encourage others to become freer in the development of their diversity and uniqueness.[30]

Loomer asks, "how big is your soul?" and along with that query, "how big is the soul of your divinity?" Small-souled persons typically have small-spirited gods?" and small-spirited images of God typically inspired small-souled theologies and behaviors. Witness in the USA, the adulation by Christians of a USA political leader as God's chosen one, despite that leader reflecting few gifts and graces and in fact denigrating the way of Christ in his personal behavior and public leadership. Our visions of God must always be larger and better than us theologically, spiritually, or ethically or they become proxies for violence and dehumanization of those who we deem to differ from us whether politically, ethnically, or sexually.

In contrast to pint-sized visions of God, Process-relational theology seeks to articulate a God of Sufficient Stature. In a fourteen-billion-year, trillion galaxy universe every vision of God is subject to critique and creative transformation. Loomer suggests that even if you claim to be "orthodox," this counts for little if your God lacks spiritual size. Process-relational theology doesn't claim to have the final word in describing God. Still, based on the interplay of our evolving and interdependent understandings of scripture (our own and others), global mysticism, tradition, reason, experience, culture, and science, the Holy One in whom all things live and move and have their being can be described as:

- *Dynamic* - constantly changing, living, dying, growing, evolving.
- *Relational* – connecting and shaping all things, whether human or non-human.
- *Experiential* – responding to all creation, from cell to soul, "feeling" the world fully as it emerges.

---

30 Harry James Cargas and Bernard Lee, (*Religious Experience and Process Theology.* Mahweh, NJ: PaulistPress. 1976), 70.

- *Pluralistic* – inspiring diversity, whether in galaxies, planets, species, humans, cultures, and religions.
- *Creative* –promoting novelty and innovation in the "adventures of ideas," science, philosophy and theology, and technology.
- *Empathetic* – despite the realities of conflict, within the evolutionary and daily survival of the fittest and natural selection, there is a movement of cooperation, complementarity, and wholes. What we experience as the "greatest" of virtues, love, is present in the simplest of realities and in the Soul of the Universe.
- *Evolving Values* – evolving values in the complexities and ambiguities of human experience, inspiring a moral and spiritual arc, shining in mystics, spiritual guides, prophets, ethical pioneers, justice seekers, and the sacrifices of everyday people, for values beyond themselves, that points to a non-coercive aim at justice and healing, tragic beauty in the universe. Our deepest values have a home in the universe, and through the ambiguity and starts and stops of history there is a horizon of hope that lures us toward God's realm on earth as it is in heaven.
- *Encircling All with Love* – going beyond the binary and exclusionary to embrace the whole universe lovingly, redemptively, and creatively, treasuring and transforming in the quest for Wholeness.

Whitehead asserts that God is the prime example of the values that shape the universe. God is also the primary inspiration in human and non-human experience for realizing these values. God's aim takes us beyond self-interest, doctrinal and spiritual exceptionalism, race, and nation, to evolving manifestations of world loyalty. God's aim is for the moment and the day in which we live, but also for the future toward which we strive. Generality of spirit and mind inspire the passionate, at times restless, quest to join this moment's fulfillment with fulfillment for all creation. Yet, beneath that restlessness is the ocean of peace that inspires Jesus, Gautama, the Bodhisattva, and the prophet.

The Quest for Generality of Experience. In this practice intended to help you "live" process-relational theology-spirituality, devote focused time for mindfulness and self-examination, asking the following questions:

- Whom do I exclude from my compassion and moral consideration?
- What realities of human experience am I excluding due to my previous life experiences or personal and social privilege?
- What parts of reality – or persons – do I perceive as "god-less," that is, bereft of spirituality or morality?
- Where do I need to expand my circle of compassion?
- What first steps might I take to embody more fully God's global vision in my daily life and citizenship?

Knowing that God is inspiring us each moment of the day, and within every encounter, we can ask in the spirit of Charles Sheldon's social gospel classic, "What would Jesus do?" or "What brings wholeness and beauty?" The Infinite present in the intimate is our companion in every choice we make, luring us to spiritual breadth and generality of consideration.

7.

The glorification of power has broken more hearts than it has healed…If the world is to find God, it must find [God] through love and not fear. [31]

Most baby boomers remember singing along to Jackie De-Shannon's "What the world needs now is love sweet love/That's the only thing there's just too little of." While the theme may seem simplistic, in many ways, the folk singer is on target theologically and ethically. Abstract theologies and ethics have left in their wake broken hearts and broken lives. Religious traditions have sanctioned murder and imprisonment for otherwise faithful people deemed heretics by religious authorities and moral potentates. Cross and sword have joined together to maintain power structures. They have aligned with the love of power rather than the power of love.

In the final chapter of *Process and the Reality,* Whitehead reflects on theological visions of God. The philosopher notes that "when the Western world accepted Christianity, Caesar conquered," supplanting the Jesus in its description of God's attributes. "The brief Galilean vision of humility flickered, uncertainly…the deeper idolatry, of the fashioning of God in the image of the Egyptian, Persian, and Roman rulers was retained. The church gave unto God the attributes that belonged exclusively to Caesar."[32]

In the marriage of church and state, then and now, power replaced love as the primary attribute of God. The church as custodian of salvation ruled by violence and inquisition. Heresy hunting replaced dialogue. Diversity of experience gave way to uniformity of doctrine. The mysticism that gave birth to Christianity was outlawed, outside of the confines of monasteries, as a threat to the church's role as direct spokesperson for God.

Power corrupts and often absolutely in the marriage of religion and politics, both of which join in claiming institutional ultimacy.

31 Ibid., 55.
32 Alfred North Whitehead, *Process and Reality: Corrected Edition* (New York: Free Press, 1978), 342.

Persons of faith align themselves with authoritarian political leaders in a mutually enriching quest for control over technology, voting rights, political policy, and women's, black, First American, and LGBTQ bodies. Televangelists and religious leaders sell their souls and the souls of their congregants for a few seats on the Supreme Court, and excuse presidential or monarchical immorality for a few crumbs at the demagogue's table. Theological and ethical abstractions, relating to doctrine, abortion, and LGBT relationships, often enforced by statutory law or doctrinal policy, replace the lived experience of God's love. Tragically, authoritarian images of God inspire – or justify – authoritarian ecclesiastical and doctrinal positions and the alignment of religious institutions with authoritarian political leaders. Power and control, and not the way of Jesus, are what matters to these religious zealots, often under the guise of saving fetuses or saving heathens from hell.

Beneath the compassionate "hate the sin love sinner" exterior of these religious crusaders is a war against women and LGBTQ and "turn or burn" for infidels and non-Christians. God's glory becomes an iron fist rather than a loving heart. As Whitehead observes, "The worship of glory arising from power is not only dangerous; it arises from a barbaric conception of God. I suppose the world itself could not contain the bones of those slaughtered because of men intoxicated by its attraction."[33] "My country right or wrong", and "my faith right or wrong", subvert the quest for beloved community.

Process-relational theologian Bernard Loomer identifies two contrasting kinds of power – unilateral power and relational power. Unilateral power, the glorification of divine and human power, speaks but does not listen. Coerces but does not cooperate. Determines but doesn't let go. It is by nature controlling, fearing that creativity and innovation by others will threaten its authority. In the zero sum world of unilateral power, power is hoarded by those who have it. Any gain by others is seen as a threat, whether these gains involve economic justice, human rights, or self-determina-

---

33 *Religion in the Making,* 54.

tion. From this perspective, any hint of human creativity threatens God's sovereignty and takes away God's power. Pluralism threatens the old-time religion of white Christian exceptionalism.

In contrast, relational power seeks partnerships and affirms other centers of power. Relational power is creative and innovative. It is also responsive, adapting to the creativity of others. Relational power sees power as ever-expanding far beyond individual and institutional self-interest. When others flourish, we flourish as well. Gains in human rights, economic wellbeing, and planetary health may challenge our current privilege and way of life, but these challenges are viewed as reflections of the ever-evolving moral and spiritual arcs of history. God is the ultimate example of relational power. When creatures are more creative, they expand the range of divine creativity and enhance the divine-human relationship. Creatures are the hands, feet, and heart of God, who nurtures companionship and co-creativity in the quest to heal the planet.

Process relational theology affirms that the aim of the universe is toward the production of beauty. Beauty emerges in supporting and affirmative environment. Beauty grows when creatures are encouraged to follow their inner wisdom and express their greatest gifts. Beauty, like power, is inherently political, in its affirmation of diversity, contrast, creativity, and freedom congruent with the common good of healthy societies. Today, in this time of pandemic and protest, we need beauty that embraces and transforms pain into wellbeing and creative transformation. We need the power of love, not the love of power.

Examining our Power. In this process-relational spiritual practice, patterned after the Ignatian Examen, we begin our time with silent openness to God's wisdom. In the quiet, listening for God's vision in our vision, we take the following reflective steps.

Giving thanks for our life and the values that sustain and nurture us.

1. From a place of gratitude, reflect on your unique privileges, emerging from your family of origin, race, ethnicity, gender, sexuality.
2. Reflect on how your privileges have shaped your understanding and use of power.
3. Consider whether you, or the institutions of which you are apart, use your power justly.
4. Consider the experiences of those who lack the privileges that you take for granted.
5. Prayerfully reflect on ways that you can let go of certain privileges and power to benefit the vulnerable and marginalized.
6. Open to God's wisdom for the future with gratitude, prepared to respond in accordance with God's vision.

8

> *Religion is world loyalty... God is that function in the world
> by reason of which our purposes are directed to ends which in
> our own consciousness are impartial to our own interests ... of
> which our purposes extend beyond values for ourselves to values
> for others.*[34]

I believe that we are all little Christs, Bodhisattvas, and Mahatmas in training. We are saints in the making. We may not know it yet, but we are part of a larger story, God's vision of planetary and interpersonal healing. The aim of the universe is toward the production of beauty, Whitehead asserts. This aim is evident not only in the evolution of galaxies and planets but in the one unrepeatable moment you are experiencing right now!

The aim of each moment, grounded in the experience of God's initial aim, is the embodiment of complexity and intensity of experience in the present and future, in the Holy Here and Now, and in the expanding circles of time and space beyond. The essential interdependence of life calls us beyond ourselves, initially in concern for the next few moments of our experience and ultimately expanding to promote the well-being of others over the long haul.

Religion is world loyalty. World loyalty begins with reflecting on our impact on others and the intimate connection between our wellbeing and the wellbeing of those around us, and then challenges us to expand our circles of concern to embrace our immediate family and acquaintances, communities, nation, and the planet. A world loyal religion goes beyond parochialism to universalism. To expand the borders of our ethics to embrace friend and foe, human and non-human, present generations and to future descendants. World loyalty involves giving up power and privilege, including the claim to the be sole repository of truth, to enhance the lives of others.

Glimpses of world loyalty are found at every level of life, from a mother bird willing to sacrifice its life to protect its chicks to a soldier going off to war or a protester risking imprisonment to

---

34   Ibid., 59, 151-152.

challenge injustice. Healthy religion calls us beyond ourselves. Our salvation is connected to the healing of others.

Jesus said that those who love their lives, focusing primarily on their own personal prosperity and wellbeing with lose their lives, while those who are willing to lose their lives for a greater good will their lives in companionship with God. The rugged individualist, concerned about their own success and prosperity, may gain the world, but they will lose their soul and everything else they hold dear.

Process theology challenges us to move from self-interest to world loyalty, recognizing that our own peace of mind and the wellbeing of our communities comes from pursuing interests larger than ourselves. The rugged self-made and self-interested person is the person most pitied by spiritual teachers and religious traditions. The individualist's soul is small and self-enclosed, unable to experience the grandeur and wonder of life. To the rugged individualist, life is a battlefield in which only the strong survive. Everything is a potential threat. Others' gain is our loss. Relationships are based on quid pro quo, getting is more important than giving. Whoever dies with the most toys wins! But you still die, and your attachment to what you cannot own or possess forever imprisons you in defensiveness, fear, and isolation.

Sacrifice is at the heart of world loyalty. Sacrifice is a global virtue, necessary for healthy communities, nations, and the planet. Grandparents sacrifice their time in getting involved in responding to gun violence, climate change, and social injustice so that they will become "good ancestors," improving the quality of life not only for their own grandchildren but for children they will never meet. Single people without children willingly pay taxes, coach sports, march in the streets, and advocate for political positions that promote the wellbeing and equity of youth and children. We are "first responders" and "essential workers" in the quest for local and global healing. We have a role no one else can replicate in God's Realm of Beauty and Love.

The survival of the planet depends on our world loyalty. Process theology encourages a theology and ethics of *ubuntu,* "I am because of you." Nation first and Christian first ideologies must give way to generous globalism. With Mother Teresa, those who walk with Whitehead are challenged to "do something beautiful for God," knowing that every act of beauty expands our souls and radiates across the universe tipping the world from death to life and hate to love.

An Exercise in World Loyalty. In this time of reflective prayer, begin with a deep calming and centering breath. Breathe gently and quietly feeling your unity with all life. Feel your connection with life that sustains you and life shaped by you. In your imagination, visualize a healing energy centering your being. Then as you breathe, expand your consciousness to include your family, neighborhood, family, nation, and the world. Connected with the whole world, then pray for guidance. Ask God to give you a sense of possibility and energy to go beyond yourself to experience world loyalty. Ask God to present you with a vision for shaping the world for the good. Thank God for an opportunity to be God's companion in healing the earth.

9.

*The whole world conspires to produce a new creation. It
presents to the creative process its opportunities and limitations.*[35]

Throughout these meditations, I have asserted that reality is
social process. The process is the reality and the reality is relationship. Relationship characterizes each moment of experience. This
is the heart of process-relational theology. The world is one vast,
interdependent organism in which each of us is a micron, each
community a cell in a dynamic, evolving universe. The apostle
Paul's vision of the "body of Christ" is more than just a poetic
image. It describes the nature of the universe as well as healthy
Christian community. God's relationship to the world can be described in terms of the world soul, the universal and ever-present
spirit of life, transcendent and inclusive of all things, yet present
within each thing as its animating principle.

When Whitehead asserts that "the whole world conspires to
produce a new creation," that is, each moment of experience, he is
proclaiming the profound interdependence without which nothing
would exist. We are all receivers and givers. Our lives, moment
by moment, emerge from our immediate environment and the
ambient universe and in its process of self-creation, each moment
leaving its mark on future moments, our own as well as creatures
near and far. In the words of poet Francis Thompson:

All things by immortal power.
 Near of far, to each other linked are,
that thou canst not stir a flower
 without troubling of a star.

The universe is a truly beloved community. To deny community is to go against the nature of things. In the body of Christ,
whether seen as the church or planet, "If one member suffers, all
suffer together with it; if one member is honored, all rejoice together with it. Now you are the body of Christ and individually

---

35 Ibid., 109.

members of it." (1 Corinthians 12:26-27) Love is, as the apostle Paul says, the binding energy of the universe, part and whole, nurturing our personal gifts and inspiring us to share our gifts with others. Love, as Dante says, moves the sun and other stars, and truly does make the world go around. Love joins the piper plover with the beach grasses and the hump backed whale with the expansive sea. Love brings children to splash in the gentle waves of Craigville Beach and their older siblings to surf the big ones in Hawaii.

Sacred and secular, one and many, mirror and interpenetrate one another. Whether we speak of race, culture, religion, or personal existence, diversity is real, and individuality is real. Each moment is unique and unrepeatable in its solitary moment of self-creation. Perspective is shaped by history, race, culture, and religion. Yet, every perspective is connected deep down with every other perspective in the intricate ecology of life. Unique in character, each moment - and dare we say each culture, race, and religion - is also the product of billions of other moments providing it energy, direction, and materials for its process of self-creation.

Individualism and relationship require and mirror each other in the ever-evolving, dynamic, and interdependent universe. God is the spiritual reality that joins all things in their diversity through God's presence in each past moment and unifies the present by the interplay of God's global and intimate vision. In the interplay of order and novelty, God is the inner spirit holding creation together.

In the spirit of holistic medicine, God's spirit is present in and shapes every bodily cell and organ, and every bodily cell and organ – moment of experience, individual, community – shapes the quality of divine experience. God's impact endures forever and cannot be threatened by any individual or cosmic negativity. Still, embodied experience is embraced by and contributes positively or negatively to God's experience.

We are profoundly relational, and the nature of our relationships limits and inspires. Without relationships, we would not exist. Yet, as we know from personal experience, the past can be the source of health or disease, and post-traumatic stress or basic trust.

Still, we are the artists of experience, who synthesize the materials of our lives in the creation of each moment and a lifetime. In the spirit of the Southern African philosophy of *ubutu,* "I am because of you," and conversely, "you are because of me," as we shape moment by moment each other's experience of reality.

The interdependence of life inspires relational ethics that take us from individuality to community and beyond self-interest to world loyalty. At the individual, communal, and national level, our calling is to go beyond individualism to affirm our responsibility to the totality. No person or nation is an island, sufficient to itself. We are all in the same storm but large-spirited souls seek in our relationships to be in the same boat, sharing each other's joys and sorrows, and obligated to seek the wellbeing of persons we will never meet. Recognizing both our limits and need for personal and national survival, our vocation is to be God's companions in healing the world by our day to day actions and political policies.

The Power of Process Affirmations. The use of positive affirmations, repeated throughout the day, focus our experience and enable us to experience the energy of divine possibility. Affirmations enable us to experience possibility in the limitations of life. Begin with a time of silence and then take a few minutes throughout the day to repeat these process-relational affirmations:

> *The limitations of the life are the source of possibility.*
> *I am connected with the Energy of the Universe.*
> *In moments of quiet, I experience God's vision for my life.*
> *God is me with possibilities for every moment of my life.*
> *I am lovingly connected with all things.*

What process-relational affirmations will add to this list, reflecting your experience of cosmic relatedness in this moment of new creation?

10.

The decay of Christianity and Buddhism, as determinative forces in modern thought is due to the fact that each religion has unduly sheltered itself from the other...instead of looking to each other for deeper meanings.[36]

We live in a pluralistic age. At a tap of our computer keyboard, we can encounter virtually limitless spiritual, cultural, and entertainment options. This has transformed our daily lives as well as our religious traditions. Unless you live off the grid, you have become a global citizen, like it or not! The rise of Nation-first and Christian Nationalist politics has occurred in good measure in reaction to the realities of ethnic, racial, and religious pluralism and changing national demographics. Many long for the "good old days" of "Father Knows Best" and "The Andy Griffith Show" – stay at home moms, male dominance, white privilege, and the simple religious menu of Protestant, Catholic, Jew. Those days are gone and will never come again, and this is good news in the evolving moral and spiritual arc of the universe.

Whitehead notes that organisms respond to the environmental changes in a variety of ways, some helpful and others dysfunctional. The first response is denial, the perceived threat is non-existent. Reality deniers say election results and global climate change are fake news: the election was stolen despite evidence to the contrary; humans can continue consuming fossil fuels without concern for the environment. Only God can destroy the planet; human behaviors are minimal in terms of climate change. Denial leads to death of religion and death of the planet.

The second response to significant environmental change is passivity and hopelessness. The threat is greater than any positive response we can make. Eventually everything we love will be destroyed by inexorable change, whether this involves aging congregations, immigrants overrunning our country, or the traditions we prize. COVID is all-powerful and we are helpless in its path.

36   Ibid., 140-141.

What we do makes no difference in our quest to heal the planet or save our lives.

A third response to unprecedented change recognizes the reality of change but deems any change a change for the worse or an enemy to challenge. This response can manifest itself in seeing religious and ethnic diversity as dangerous, and unwelcome in our communities. In the world of fundamentalist and authoritarian theology, other religious traditions or differing forms of Christianity are viewed as demonic distortions of the truth or half-truths that have nothing to teach us.

A final path in responding to environmental novelty is the way of adventure and stature, involving initiating novelty to respond to novelties in our environment. While change and pluralism may threaten former certainties, traditions, and privileges, these upheavals are also opportunities for creative transformation, expanding our horizons, and rethinking our faith. The scientific adventure, whether in displacing the earth as the center of the universe, affirming a multi-billion-year evolutionary journey, or explaining certain behaviors (for example, depression, bi-polarity) in terms of chemical reactions rather than ethical decisions, can put at risk inflexible doctrines and unassailable authorities and world views. They can also deepen our understanding of the human adventure and our faith traditions.

My life is a testimony to creative transformation due to encountering the gifts of other religious traditions. I am an active Christian today due to learning Transcendental Meditation, a Hindu-based meditative technique, as a first-year college student. My understanding of Jesus' healings has expanded through encounters with complementary and global medicine, that inspired me to learn Reiki healing touch in the 1980s and a few years later become a Reiki Master Teacher. My studies of Buddhism, Hinduism, Judaism, and indigenous American, European, and African religions have deepened my sense of God's presence in the non-human world and the cycles of nature. Inter-spirituality, joining Christian and non-Christian spiritual practices, as well as my immersion in quantum physics and cosmology has expanded my understanding of God's creative wisdom in a trillion galaxy universe. I have discovered that the Intimate is also the Infinite.

Early Christian theologians proclaimed that in Christ, the true light enlightens all persons and that wherever Truth is present, God is its source. Followers of Jesus can open to God's presence in scientific laboratories and fossil digs, Mars Rovers and the Webb Telescope, Zen monasteries and counseling sessions, in taking our medications as well as practicing meditation.

Although Christianity and Buddhism are different in many ways, we can learn from each other. Christians can learn walking and breath prayer from Vietnamese Buddhist monk, Thich Nhat Hanh, and Buddhists can recognize the importance political activism from the Hebraic prophets and the Social Gospel movement. We can forge common paths in responding to climate change, racism and economic injustice, and gun violence. We can pray and meditate together, sharing the insights of the "living Buddha" and "living Christ." Christians can learn from Buddhists non-attachment and Buddhists can learn from Christian and Jews prophetic restlessness. In our sharing, our mutual lights join and give greater light to our wayward world.

Walking with Jesus, Buddha, and Socrates. In are world of process, movement opens us to the movements of the divine in our lives. Movement inspires imagination and softens inflexibilities. This book was born in the walking. In taking passages from Whitehead's writing for a walk, after preparing the path in reading and reflection, and then opening to emerging thoughts, intuitions, and feelings. Much that happened on these process walks is indescribable: oneness with sea, shore, and sky; scudding cloud and daydreams; remembrances of dear friends deceased and heartfelt love for my family and friends; a sense of the swift passage of time and the presence of eternity.

In this exercise, take the passage which begins this chapter or another passage from this text for a walk. Let the words inspire, and then let go of control. Let thoughts, intuitions, fantasies, inspirations, music, and synchronicity emerge. You may wish to jot down a few insights, paint, draw, write a poem, or sing a song to memorialize this Moving Moment.

11.

The power by which God sustains the world is the power of himself as the ideal…the world lives by its incarnation of God in itself.[37]

Jesus once stated that his mission was that everyone, without exception, would achieve abundant life (John 10:10). Whitehead understands God's role in our lives in a similar fashion. God's power is that of pointing us toward fulfillment and liveliness in the present moment and the immediate, if not long term, future in terms of our environmental context. God is present everywhere, and in all persons and things, aiming each thing and all things in relationship toward one another toward the best possibilities for the moment. There is no Godless place nor is any place bereft of the touch of divine revelation. The ideal for each moment is not an abstraction, but an array of possibilities congruent with this place and time. God aims at what is best for us, not seeking punishment, retribution, or destruction, but fullness of life, although there are times in which the best possibility may lead to protest and confrontation.

John's Prologue asserts that "the true light that enlightens everyone was coming in the world." (John 1:5) While we may turn away from God's light, preferring self-interest, chaos, and moral darkness, God light still shines in us, moving quietly and persistently to provide healthy and world-supporting paths forward.

This morning as I walked at sunrise on a Cape Cod beach, it was easy to affirm that the world lives by the incarnation of God. I walked, in the spirit of a Navajo prayer, with beauty all around me. Every step invited me to wonder. Every breath on this chilly winter morning inspired me to equanimity and compassion. It was a morning to embrace the "ideal," a world of peace, beauty, and goodness, where people follow their best selves. Yet, when I checked NPR Morning News on my drive returning home, I was confronted by the glaring reality that much of the world is in chaos: science

---

37   Ibid., 149.

deniers and white supremacists abound motivated by hate and division; children are dying of malnutrition; a lone right whale, one of only 400 on the planet, dies in a fishing net; and hate speech and disinformation characterize social media communication. Where can we find the ideal in such situations? Where is God's incarnation to be found amid such moral ambiguity and chaos? Have we as a species turned away from the divine ideal to follow the devices and desires of our own self-interest and nation-first ideologies?

Yet, God persists. The ideal motivates social transformation and sacrificial behavior. Our sense that life can be different emerges from the impact of God's ideal, the still small voice of possibility arising in the maelstrom of personal and political complexities. God's dream of Shalom flickers throughout history but the "adventures of ideas," the horizon of possibility draws us forward, revealing the contrast between what is and what can be. In human experience, God's ideal is the source of individual conscience and prophetic protest. God's vision of possibility energizes our protesting gun violence, climate change, structural injustice and racism, political divisiveness, and unequal distribution of medical and educational resources in a time of pandemic.

Without God's ideal, the world would plunge into chaos and entropy. Apathy and self-interest would be the norm in human behavior. Social healing would be a phantasm. Although God's ideal is countered throughout national history and individual decision-making, the moral and spiritual arcs draw us forward. Wayward as we are, God is out to love us, to heal us, and not punish or abandon us.

The Gospel of Thomas says, "cleave the wood and I am there." (77) Jesus says, "you are the light of the world." (Matthew 5:14-15). For those whose "doors of perception" have been cleansed, God is, as the joke relates, "like Elvis, you'll see God everywhere!" We can experience God everywhere precisely because God is incarnate everywhere. God is incarnate in you, awaiting your seeing and then your being light to the world.

Without ideals, hope dies. Without ideals, protest and reform languish. Without ideals, the status quo in its violence and injustice is unquestioned. God is the source of restlessness and peace; protest and prayer; resistance and equanimity, pushing our world forward toward the horizons of loving possibility and global community.

Practice Seeing and Being the Light. At the inauguration of President Joe Biden and Vice-President Kamala Harris, many were touched by the poetry of Amanda Gorman, wise beyond her years. Touched by the divine muse, she reminded a listening nation to have the courage to see the light and be the light. Her words resonate with the heart of process-relational theology and spirituality. We can see the light in all things because God's light shines through all things. We can be the light because God's light can shine through us and we can point that light to others. You are the light of the world, let your light shine, as Jesus proclaims.

In this practice, open your eyes throughout the day. Look for the light in all you see. Look for the revealing of divine light in the persons you meet. Look beyond superficialities to see a deeper light flowing in and through them. In your interactions, nurture albeit subtly and quietly the presence of light in them.

Look for the light flowing in and through you, moment by moment and over a lifetime. Observe your own inner glow, the flow of insight and inspiration. Recognize that you are not only a co-creator with God, you are also a co-revealer. Reveal in gentle and unassuming ways divine light of possibility and community. Intentionally seek to bring light to every situation, including those which are most challenging to you. See divine light, be divine light, expand divine light.

12.

God confronts the actual with what is possible for it...Every
act leaves the world with a deeper or fainter impress of God. He
then passes in his next relationship to the world with enlarged, or
diminished, presentation of ideal values.[38]

God's presence in the world embraces past, present, and future.
God's activity, vision, and ethical and spiritual arcs are concrete
not abstract. God is the author of real spirituality for real people
and embodied ethics for real life decision makers. God is both the
ultimate idealist, imagining the Reign of Shalom and Healing "on
earth as it is in heaven" and the most intimate relativist, addressing
each one of us with possibilities for our current life situation and
context.

The divine relativity, described by process theologian Charles
Hartshorne, is the ongoing call and response of God's relationship
with the world. God addresses each moment of experience with
possibilities for the immediate moment and in terms of the larger
community and planetary context. God goes big, addressing the
vast expanses of cosmic and earth history. God has visions for our
whole life and our world, and they are lived out in moment by
moment divine call and creaturely response. God also thinks small,
touching each moment with creative wisdom and wise possibility.

Our responses shape God's experience of the world. We can
give God beauty or ugliness of experience by what we do today
and in this unrepeatable Holy Here and Now. Our aim should be,
as Mother Teresa counsels, to "do something beautiful for God"
both as our gifts to God and as the materials for God's further
involvement in our world.

"Every act leaves a deeper or fainter impress of God." Everything we do reveals or hides, and expands or diminishes, the
embodiment of the moral and spiritual arcs of history. While God
never gives up on anyone of us or the communities and nations of
which we are apart, certain actions deviate from God's vision for us

38   Ibid., 153, 152.

and require God to adjust God's plans for our lives and communities. Rioters lawlessly storming the USA Capitol diminish in real time God's dream of a "more perfect union" embodying "liberty and justice for all." When honest citizens and politicians confront with strong and loving moral and political power the lawless behaviors, incivility, and racism, the bad intentions, of some of our fellow citizens, these honest citizens' prayerful protests and quest for equal justice inject new possibilities for the incarnation of God's hopes for our nation. God is the world's companion, the soul of the world, the spirit of life, feeling every movement and responding to every intention. For God and for us, the future is open and undecided. Though God is the wellspring of possibilities, both rooted in eternity and emerging in the unity of ideal and concrete, God, like ourselves, is also "making it up as God goes along." Yet, God's reservoir of energy, patience, love, wisdom, and power enables us in the historical and personal adventure to "make a way where there is no way."

A living God is a loving and flexible God. A dynamic divinity is constantly changing course, blending God's mercies that are every morning with God's constancy in love and purpose. God is faithful through all the changes of our lives and God's fidelity is intimate addressed to the junction of life as it is and life and life as it could be. Accordingly, while God mourns the loss of certain possibilities and the pain people experience, God continues to respond to the world "with enlarged, or diminished, presentation of ideal values." God still responds to our deepest needs, often unknown to us.

Can you imagine the diminished possibilities that have occurred during this time of pandemic? Lives cut off prematurely. Science denial and the politicization of masks. Small businesses closing. Politicians swaying public opinion with blatant dishonesty. Can you imagine God's pain at the rise of childhood and youth depression due to isolation from their classmates in this time of pandemic? Can you fathom how much national potential has been lost by the undemocratic verbiage and actions of USA political leaders, and there "big lie" and incitement of national division? Can you fathom the potentialities diminished by the death of Breonna Taylor, the victim of police violence, and Brian Sicknick, the USA Capitol police officer killed in the line of duty during the terrorist assault on January 6? God mourns and weeps, as Jesus did over Jerusalem. Yet, in the crosses of daily life, God still injects healing possibilities within the pain and hopelessness.

Can you also imagine the divine rejoicing at persons exploring new ways of worship and teaching, the compassion and sacrifice of first responders, empathetic leadership, and financial and in-person generosity in this time of pandemic? Can you imagine the divine delight at children inventing new games and parents spending more time with their children? Can you imagine God's affirmation of churches and civic groups responding to the cry that "Black Lives Matter" and starting groups studying the many dimensions of racial and economic privilege? God is able to inject new and creative possibilities as a result of these initiatives.

What we do matters in the ongoing adventure of human experience and national life. We are God's hands and feet and co-workers in God's quest for beauty and healing. God's healing of the world needs our commitment, our imperfect yet important role in reconciliation, comfort, protest, and sacrifice for the greater good so that God's impact our lives and world will be enlarged and radiate from sea to shining sea and pole to pole and across every land with hope of adventures to come.

Opening to Ideals. It was my practice to integrate spiritual practices with my morning beach walk. As I turned back toward home, eventually I saw the steeple of the church I pastored on the horizon. Seeing the steeple was a prayer prompt for me: I took a moment as I walked to focus on the steeple, praying for the members of the congregation, those who enter the church, persons touched by the church, and the quality of my ministry with this Cape Cod faith community. When I was working in my church study, I paused when bells hourly tolled, praying for my work and the congregation's wellbeing, and particular individuals within the congregation.

In the spirit of Gerald May's prayer pattern, I believe that opening to divine possibility is a matter of pausing, noticing, opening, yielding and stretching, and then responding. Opening to divine possibility, bringing God's vision from the unconscious "sighs too deep for words" to conscious experience and activity is a matter of noticing and opening, then enhancing God's ideals by positively embracing them in our unique moment by moment self-creation.

Throughout the day, "live" process-relational theo-spirituality by opening to possibility, opening to the ideal of the moment. Breathe in possibility, noticing the vision of the moment. See possibilities in those you encounter. Ask, seek, and knock, "show me your vision, O God," and then patiently wait. We can ask God to "show me the way forward" if we have particular long- term issues confronting us.

Two years ago, as I sauntered along the beach, I recall thinking about the possibility of big changes in our family's life, involving leaving my congregation after eight years, possibly retiring from full-time ministry, and returning with my son and his family to Washington DC. My beach prayers involved listening for God's vision of long-term possibilities related to life in the Capitol area. "God, show me the way forward? Guide me toward a positive future in our new home?" Then, I listened, as possibilities emerged relating to the concrete realities of the present and future.

What objects call you to prayer? What places inspire concern for the world? Take time to pause, ask, notice, and respond to divine inspiration throughout the day.

13.

Morality of outlook is conjoined with generality of outlook...
Religion is the translation of general ideas into particular thoughts,
particular emotions, particular purposes; it is directed to the end of
stretching individual interest beyond its self-defeating particularity.[39]

At the heart of process-relational theology, and Whitehead's
cosmological vision, is the polar unity of the macrocosm and the
microcosm, the infinite and the intimate, the abstract and the concrete, and the universal and the personal. In a relational universe,
all the polarities of life are ultimately joined and require each other
to be fully understood.

Process-relational theology sees spiritual growth, theological
insight, and ethical wisdom as grounded in the widest possible
vistas of experiential reflection. Philosophers, theologians, and lay-
persons are called to be as large spirited as possible, looking for
divine revelation in the "all and the everything." Cosmopolitan in
perspective, we affirm our nation and faith as vehicles of truth and
goodness, and affirm that other faiths and nations are repositories
of truth and goodness and have something of value to contribute to
us. Fidelity to family, faith, and country opens, rather than closes,
us to the diverse manifestations of divine creativity and biological
and cultural evolution. My love for my grandchildren sensitizes me
to the pain, and activates my concern, for children who are neglect-
ed by their parents, malnourished children, or children separated
unnecessarily from the parents by governmental actions.

Generality of interest finds its fulfillment and ultimate meaning in its application to concrete actualities. The general and
particular and the macro and micro are symbiotically related and
require each other. Whitehead speaks of cosmological and scientific
discovery as being like the flight of an airplane – perhaps today it
would be the shuttle circling the earth – which:

---

39 Alfred North Whitehead, *Process and Reality: Corrected Edition* (New
York: Free Press, 15), 1978. [originally published 1929.]

Starts from the ground of particular observation [in religion, this would be the reality mystical experience or ethical
observation]; it makes the flight to the thin air of generalization
[discerning divinity and deeper moral principles present in
our experiences]; and then it again lands for acute observation
rendered acute by rational interpretation.[40]

The journey of theological and spiritual discovery is a constant
movement from the mystic's immediacy joining us with all creation
and then the marriage of mysticism with everyday reality, and once
more return to the wellsprings of mysticism and universality. Jesus is transfigured on the mountaintop but must then return to
the flatlands, responding the pleas of a father for his critically ill
child. Muhammed must leave the cave to walk the streets of Mec-
ca, bringing his vision of monotheism and morality to governance
and business practices. Mother Theresa's sense of divine guidance
leads her minister to the forgotten dying on the streets of Calcutta
despite her long-term depression.

Generality without particularity becomes abstract. Generality,
especially in ethics, must be tested in concrete personal experiences.
Loyalty to nation is tested in gazing at the faces of children separated from their parents on our nation's borderlands. Sexual mores
are tested in encounters with the LGBTQ community. Attitudes
toward abortion and euthanasia are refined in relationships with
people living with unnecessary suffering and women struggling to
make the right decision in terms of carrying a fetus to term. Then,
conversely, particularity without generality leads to nation first,
white supremacy, Christian nationalism, narcissistic decision-making, and simplistic ethical judgments. We need to look beyond
our own self and national interest to wider horizons of value and
obligation.

Generality of outlook is essential for moral decision-making
and public policy in today's dynamically changing interdependent
world. No nation, religion, community, or person can go it alone.
We need to think globally, even as we act locally. We must look

---

40   Ibid., 5.

generations ahead as we plan for the here and now. Rejoicing in the beauty of the day, our calling is also to be "good ancestors" who commit to responsible behaviors in relationship to generations we will never meet.

The Spirit of Generality. Today, we need to consider what it means to be a "good ancestor." Most people reading this text will be adults, many of whom are parents and grandparents, or significant others for children and youth. Our challenge is to live in the now and make plans for the future of children and youth. In the interdependence of life, our actions radiate across space and time, shaping the lives of our descendants. We will be part of the universe that shapes their experience. Consider the impact of your life today on the economic and environmental future of generations ahead. Taking time to contemplate the interplay of your current situation and the future, what actions can you take to ensure a positive future for future generations? How can you live more simply so others can simply live? How is your lifestyle related to the sustainability of the planet? Make a commitment to embrace a process-relational view of reality as you prioritize your personal and political decision-making.

14.

God is the organ of novelty aiming at intensification....God's purpose in the creative advance is the evocation of intensities.[41]

I grew up singing "Give me that old time religion/It was good for my mother/It was good for my father/It's good enough for me" in the Baptist church of my youth. The lyrics and tune were catchy, especially at our revival meetings and singspirations.[42] I honor the faith of my parents, the Baptist church of my childhood, the wisdom of scripture, the insights of the Hebraic prophets, the apostles, and over two thousand years of Christian reflection and spiritual experience. I wouldn't be here, as a process theologian, without the values and love of scripture I learned as a child.

I also recognize that holding on to that old time religion has often led to clinging to the status quo – to accepting slavery as God's will, seeing civil rights and the social gospel as a betrayal of the Gospel, condemning science as demonic, and pronouncing eternal damnation on persons outside Christianity. These days, holding onto the old time religion has tragically been connected with opposing women's rights, ostracizing the LGBTQ community, and aligning with authoritarian political leaders.

Whitehead recognizes the importance of the past in shaping persons and institutions. Tradition provides the "playing field" for faith development, the boundaries for change, a sense of identity, and guardrails to maintain a sense of spiritual integrity. When held too tightly, however, tradition can stifle innovation and silence contrasting voices. Whitehead notes that we can no more hold onto unchanging tradition, than we can, to quote the Pre-Socratic philosopher Heraclitus, step in the same waters twice. The pure conservative, fighting against change, is going against the nature of the universe.

---

41 Ibid., 67, 105.
42 A "singspiration" is a gathering to sing old hymns, hear the gospel preached, meet friends, and eat good food.

To the consternation of those who see change as a fall from grace and the one true faith, God is, Whitehead believes, the organ of novelty. God is the ultimate source of cosmic, planetary, human, institutional, and ethical evolution. In the call and response of the creative process, God is the energetic wisdom that propels the universe forward. Working within the materials of creation, the energies of life, described by Whitehead as Creativity, God moves the world upward, forward, inward, and outward. God inspires the emergence of galaxies and the "adventures of ideas" of human philosophical, theological, scientific, and ethical advancement. As organ of novelty, God is the motive force of the evolutionary process, operative in the causal relatedness that often appears chaotic, random, and competitive in nature. Like the heart or the brain, God is the life-giving presence, the source of dependable structures as well as imaginative alternatives.

God's mercies are new every morning. Each day brings a new creation. The orderliness of life finds fulfillment as foundation for innovation and adventure. The structures of the social order are enlivened and challenged by prophetic restlessness, that strives to transform the old order, cutting away the inessential and unjust, so that the light of God's new order will shine on all God's children.

The reality of divine novelty, the universal and personal quest for complexity and intensity, beauty and justice, and discovery and adventure, pushes us forward toward new ethical and spiritual horizons. God is the source of prophetic restlessness and the peace that surpasses personality and lures us from self-interest and nation-first to horizons of sacrificial living, justice-seeking, and world loyalty. Wherever there is creative transformation, we will, as process theologian John Cobb asserts, discover Christ's presence whether on the picket line, in a laboratory, in the clash of ideas, in the meditation hall, gazing at the night sky, or overcoming alienation. Not locked into past achievements, God constantly reminds us "behold, I am doing a new thing" and challenges us to claim our place as God's companions in imagining new visions of human life and our place in the cosmos and then embodying these transforming visions in the daily life of our families, communities, nation, and planet.

Embracing Holy Adventure. Adventure is at the heart of process-relational theology and spirituality. It is baked into the universe and whether we embrace it or not, our lives are adventures into the unknown and unexpected. Even high control persons could not have expected the impact of the pandemic nor can we fully determine the course of our personal health, professional success, and family wellbeing. We are agents of our destiny but our agency is often shaped by unexpected adventures. We can lean into adventure, adapting and innovating, or we can deny it. We can rejoice in on-line classes and worship or bemoan lack of in-person worship. We can see mask wearing as prayerful and compassionate or an intrusion on our liberty, an example of fake science. We can reshape our values in accordance with new insights on racial, economic, and gender privilege and climate change or we can go on with "business as usual," complicit in injustice and environmental destruction.

In a time of national challenge, the prophet Isaiah heard God's voice, alerting him to adventure ahead. Isaiah was about to embark on a holy adventure – and call his compatriots to adventure – in companionship with the Holy Adventurer.

> Do not remember the former things,
>> or consider the things of old.
> I am about to do a new thing;
>> now it springs forth, do you not perceive it?
> I will make a way in the wilderness
>> and rivers in the desert. (Isaiah 43:18-19)

God is doing a new thing, and so should we in response to God's call. Knowing that God is the organ of novelty, the inspiration to creative transformation, in this spiritual practice, begin with a time of silence, followed by reading Isaiah 43:18-19 (above). Let the words soak in as they speak of letting go and moving forward. What images of the future come to mind? Toward what destination do you see God's Holy Adventure luring you? What do you need to let go of to open to God's future? From time to time come back to this scripture and the interplay of letting go and moving forward. When it is appropriate, take actions to embrace God's holy adventure moving through your life.

15.

We find in the first two lines of a famous hymn a full expression of the two notions [permanence and change] in one integral experience:

> *Abide with me*
> *Fast falls the eventide.*[43]

Cosmology inspires poetry as well as spirituality. Whitehead the philosopher-poet describes two polarities of experience. The first is "all things flow." Time passes. The infant grows into the child, the teen, the young adult, the parent in midlife, the grandparent in retirement, and then the pilgrim toward eternity. Now in my seventies, I feel the brevity of life. It seems like yesterday that I was playing little league baseball and falling in love for the first time. Now, I look toward the possibility of retirement, and though I feel forever young, I don't run cross country these days, and hold onto the rail when I go down the stairs. I rejoice in a good walk on the beach as the pinnacle of my exercise routine. Life is "perpetual perishing," Whitehead muses. A lifetime passes in the blink of an eye. The greatest evil, the philosopher confesses, is the passage of immediacy into memory. The loss of the present must be embraced to give way to possibilities of the future.

The hymn, "Abide with me/Fast falls the eventide" reveals life's brevity, and also points to the permanent elements of life – "the solid earth, the mountains, the stones, the Egyptian Pyramids, the spirit of [humankind], God."[44] Every evening and before sunrise, I have rituals that shape my spirituality. Before I retire, I go outside and gaze at the heavens, reflecting on the immensity of the cosmic journey, a universe of trillions of stars, nearly fourteen billion years in the making. I am filled with awe. I do the same as I awaken before dawn, marveling at divine handiwork and giving thanks for the wonder of all being and a new day filled with possibility and

---

43   Ibid., 208-209.
44   Ibid., 208.

adventure. Yet, this sense of eternity is also shaped, especially in this time of COVID, by my evening prayers in which I ask God to preserve me through the night and awaken me to the new day with vigor and creativity.

The fluidity and impermanence of life are beyond my control. I depend on the liveliness of new possibilities, but adventure depends on letting go of the present moment. The moment perishes, gives way to the next, and lives evermore.

God is the ultimate repository of permanence and change. Throughout this text, I have alluded to the wisdom of Lamentations 3:22-24 as capturing the faithfulness of the everchanging, everlasting God:

> The steadfast love of the LORD never ceases,
>> his mercies never come to an end;
> they are new every morning;
>> great is your faithfulness.
>
> "The LORD is my portion," says my soul,
>> "therefore I will hope in him." (Lamentations 3:22-24)

The Most Faithful is the most changeable. The Most Eternal is the most dynamic. Novelty is the ultimate witness to fidelity and steadfastness. The eternal and all-encompassing Vision of God, described as the Primordial Nature of God, grounds the world of change, containing the vast array of foundational possibilities (described by Whitehead as Eternal Objects) and giving birth to new constellations of possibility. The everlasting life of God embraces and responds to the ongoing universe, constantly changing, yet fully preserving the ever-changing universe. Everything that exists, in its rising and perishing, eventually receives "objective immortality," in the ever-evolving and ever-expanding memory of God, God's consequent nature. God's integration of eternity and time flows back into the world as God's responsive love, joining call and response, giving birth to new possibilities and the energy to embody these in the ongoing transformation of the universe.

We are part of the amazing integrity and innovation of flux and permanence. Our own personal artistry is our gift to the universe beyond ourselves, dynamically donating our lives to the universe that emerges with each moment of experience, with confidence that we can do something beautiful for God and play our part in healing the universe. Our passing acts will live forevermore in God's memory.

The eternal meaning of our lives gives value in a world of change. What we do matters. What we do makes a difference. Our lives are our gifts to God, providing God with the materials for new creation in the ongoing evolution of the planet.

Embracing Eternity and Change. In this spiritual practice, we explore the polarities of permanence and flux. After a period of silence, spend a few minutes reading and reflecting on Lamentations 3:22-24 (above). Let the words and images elicited by the scripture flow in and through you as you ponder the interplay of permanence and flux, and trust and change. Upon what realities do you depend? What realities are trustworthy in your life? What realities are stable in your life? In contrast, what is in flux and uncertain? Where do you experience God in the changes of life? Visualize life flowing through you toward the future with God as your dynamic future. Give thanks for God's faithfulness as you commit the future to God's wisdom, asking for guidance through all life's changes.

16.

The initial aim is rooted in the nature of God... The initial aim is the best for that impasse. But if the best be bad, then the ruthlessness of God can be personified as Ate, the goddess of mischief. The chaff is burnt.[45]

This passage is one of my favorites in the Whiteheadian corpus. It is also one of the most challenging for those who say "God is in control." I often invoke "the best for that impasse" in administrative contexts where less than perfect decisions need to be made. I share my belief that "there are many right responses and I think this is the best one at this moment." I remind my friends that in family life, organizational decision-making, and public and political policy we need to fix our eyes on the far horizon of possibility, the ideals that draw us forward, and recognize "the power of the penultimate," achieving something good when the ideal is currently beyond our reach.

This passage scandalizes people who believe that God determines every event as God chooses. It suggests that limits are placed on God as well as us. That God must contend with the real world of real decision-makers and real histories, and must choose concrete options that can be achieved rather than abstract options that are ultimate and ideal. It also suggests that in certain historical moments, the highest values we can achieve may be painful to ourselves and others. While we have an obligation to seek reconciliation in certain situations of personal conflict, we also may have to resort to various levels of coercion to protect the interests of vulnerable persons. Criminals may need to be jailed to protect the community. Rioters at the USA Capitol need to be restrained and handcuffed to protect our democracy and members of Congress, families, and staff. Boycotts of businesses and bus lines need to be called to achieve voting rights and equal treatment for African Americans in the United States. Our quest for the "more perfect union" may require step-by-step achievements, grounded in the interplay of

45 Ibid., 244.

idealism and compromise. When we can't sing "Kum-Ba-Yah," we may need to confront, challenge, criticize, and compel structural and interpersonal injustices. The prophets of Israel threaten political and religious catastrophe in response to the nation's injustice. Failure to hear the cries of the poor leads to a "famine" of hearing God's word. God is still working for justice and redemption, for empathy among the wealthy and powerful, but their continued injustice and apathy blocks the full articulation of divine possibility.

God works within every situation. God's power is primarily relational, and seldom, if at all, coercive. God envisions and works toward the Realm of Shalom but must work with us to achieve this vision. Accordingly, God is the ultimate relativist as well as the ultimate pragmatist. God needs us to be God's hands, feet, minds, and hearts to help achieve God's vision of truth, beauty, and goodness in the world. God loves us and the world personally and concretely, not abstractly, and provides in each moment the highest values for our wellbeing and growth, contingent on our responses.

God aims high and so should we. God looks toward the far horizon and so should we. God lures us forward with the spiritual and moral arcs of history, challenging, energizing, and inspiring, and we should follow God's way and have our "eyes on the prize." This may mean prophetic protest and entering the arena of competing powers. In the meantime, God challenges us to hold in contrast God's ultimate goals for history and the penultimate possibilities available in real life political situations, moving forward one step at a time in the quest for personal, relational, and social justice and healing.

Pragmatic Progressivism. God wants us to settle for "more," not "less." God seeks abundant life for a creation. Although ideal possibilities are ambient, divine abundance always involves achieving the best possibility for the current situation. This means keeping your eyes on the prize and moving forward one step at a time. The challenge is to have the insight to embrace the best possibility rather than sacrificing the "good" that is available for the currently unavailable "ideal." Following Whitehead's reflection on the aims of the living organisms to first "live" and then live "well" and finally to live "better," personally and politically we seek to constantly open ourselves to higher values, starting where we are and moving forward toward open horizons of fulfillment.[46]

Opening to the "best for that impasse" involves mindfulness or self-awareness, grounded in the reality that despite the circumstances of life, we always are able to use our freedom creatively and lovingly. Even in the worst circumstances, we have, as psychiatrist and Holocaust survivor Viktor Frankl says, the ability to frame our attitude toward the events of our lives. This requires a sense of agency and awareness to observe what is possible and act accordingly.

Awareness of options is a matter of spiritual discernment over the long haul and moment by moment. After you have centered yourself – with breath, prayer, music, or movement – then observe what is going on in your life and environment. Explore the possibilities available to you deliberately, if possible, or briskly, if necessary. Ask, and then wait for an answer to the question, "What is the best in this situation? What is my best behavior option?" Let this practice shape your decision-making process, enabling you to choose wisely between the array of possibilities in any given situation.

---

46 Alfred North Whitehead, *The Function of Reason* (Boston: Beacon Press, 1929), 8.

17.

*When the Western world accepted Christianity, Caesar con-
quered... The brief Galilean vision of humility, uncertainly... the
Galilean vision...does not emphasize the ruling Caesar or the
ruthless moralist, or the unmoved mover. It dwells upon the tender
elements of the world which slowly and in quietness operate by love;
and it finds its purpose in the present immediacy of a kingdom
not of this world. Love neither rules, nor is it unmoved; also it is
a little oblivious to morals. It does not look to the future; but finds
its own reward in the immediate present.*[47]

God is love, and Jesus is the incarnation of divine love. Love
is powerful, and ideally the best use of human power is loving.
Jesus had great power, the power of inclusion, hospitality, healing,
justice, and love. In contrast to dictators and demagogues, Jesus
believed in shared power. He told his followers that they could do
greater things than he did as they taught his message of Shalom to
the wider world. Jesus had a global vision and this global vision was
incarnate in concrete personal relationships. Jesus did not follow
the abstract "one size fits all" policy in spirituality, ethics, or healing. He encountered living, breathing struggling people in search
of more abundant life and gave them a blessing unique to their
needs. In the spirit of the process-relational God, Jesus provided his
followers with imaginative and transformational possibilities and
the energy to achieve them. Jesus "breathed" on the women and
men, gathered in an upper room, conveying God's Spirit to them,
thus placing the future of his ministry in their hands.

Yet, as Christianity grew from politically persecuted to politically powerful, it adapted to the ways of Caesar, hoarding power,
requiring obedience, and persecuting outsiders and persons with alternative understandings of faith. The faith of the martyrs morphed
into the perpetrator of martyrdom for those who fell outside its
narrow norms. The church became the motive force behind coloni-
zation, joining subjugation with salvation. The way of healing and

---

47   *Process and Reality.*, 342-343.

the promise of eternal life was restricted to priests and sacraments. Power-hungry prelates proclaimed, "outside the church there is no salvation." The simple healing hospitality of the Galilean was lost in the process.

Caesarian and Constantinian Christianity recognized that institutional survival requires the use of power, but it made the acquisition and maintaining of power an end unto itself, forgetting that it is Love that guides the galaxies, stars, and human heart. Love endures forever, while the Caesars, Napoleons, Stalins, Putins, and Trumps strut and fret, bloviating and bombarding, have their day, destructive as it may be, and then depart the stage of history.

Readers of Whitehead have been puzzled that a philosopher so concerned with ethics and values would suggest that the Galilean vision is "a little oblivious to morals." God's moral and spiritual vision propels history forward. God's vision, however, is personal and not abstract. It is about quality of experience, and beauty and complexity of experience and impact on the future, not inflexible rules or doctrines. Inflexible and abstract ethical and moral principles fail to consider the needs and values, and the challenges and temptations, of real persons, and when meted out without consideration of human experience serve to stifle rather than expand the impact of God's vision our lives and in history.

God's morality is personal, grounded God's immersion in the world as the Most Moved Mover, as Charles Hartshorne asserts. God knows our weakness and strength, anxiety and hope, and addresses us personally. Likewise, while interpersonal ethics and public policy need guideposts to ensure justice and order, ethics and public policy are intended to join zest, adventure, creativity, freedom, responsibility, and integrity in the quest for beauty in the moment, in shaping communities, and in the long vista of planetary history.

The Spirit of the Now. In the present moment, the impact of the past and the lure of the future meet. The weight of the past gives birth to limitation and possibility. To be healthy as persons and communities, we must come to terms with the past – its joys and traumas, the quest for freedom and the burden of the slavery. Letting go of the past's domination requires agency, creativity, and forgiveness. It requires honor and healing. Opening to the call of the future requires allowing the past to be a catalyst and not a cage. In this Holy Here and Now, we can experience freedom, joy, creativity, and novelty as well as pain and conflict, as pathways to the promise of the future.

The immediate present is the moment of wholeness and transformation. The Holy Here and Now is the moment of decision. As a spiritual practice, simply observe your responses moment by moment, noting the blending of past and future in this present moment. Not locked in the past but seeing the past as the source of future transformation - the painful and joyful palette of experiences with which you create "tragic beauty" in this Holy Moment. In this Holy Moment, you can pray with United Nations Secretary General Dag Hammarskjold:

> For all that has been – thanks!
> For all that shall be – yes!

18.

*The consequent nature of God is [God's] judgment. [God]
saves the world and it passes into the immediacy of God's own life.
It is the judgement of a tenderness which loses nothing that can
be saved. It is the judgement of a wisdom which uses what in the
temporal world is mere wreckage...God's role is not the combat
of productive force with productive force, of destructive force with
destructive force; it lies in the patient operation of the overpowering
rationality of [God's] conceptual harmonization. [God] does not
create the world, [God] saves it: or more accurately, he is the poet
of the world with tender patience leading it by [his] vision of truth,
beauty, and goodness.*[48]

God is a poet? God is an artist? God is a storyteller and novelist? God posts urban murals and tags walls? God as an opera singer and rapper? God as a ballerina and metal sculptor? God as singer and songwriter? God makes sand castles on the beach and sand paintings in a healing ceremony?

Not our usual images of God. If we prefer a kinder, gentler god, we see God as "father" or "mother" or "companion." If we like a more "robust," though often brittle god, we exalt the "king," "sovereign," and "all-powerful One." But God is also an artist and poet and dancer. God loves Beethoven and Beyonce, Brahms, the Beatles, and the Beach Boys. God inspires Rilke and Rumi and Rachmaninoff. God writes in Russian as well as Hebrew, Diné as well as English.

There are many images of the divine, emerging from human creativity and imagination, from experiences of holiness, both from the human and non-human worlds. God is also described as a "mother hen," "eagle," "rock," "fire," and "wind."

Whitehead's image of God as poet points to God's working with the materials of creation, guided by a vision, to bring forth something novel and wonderful. Poets create with something, rather than out of nothing. Artists use materials to bring new pos-

48 Ibid., 346.

sibilities into the world. Words, paint, canvas, voice, flesh and bone, notes and scales, and the previous insights of other artists, poets, and writers.

Whitehead believes that poetry best describes God's vision. As a writer, I trust the intuitive spirit that inspires poets. I let insights and intuitions, sights and sounds, and the words of others flow in and through me, bringing something new into the world, something reflective of global wisdom and personal insight. I have a vision that guides my writing. In the case of this book, making process theology come alive as an experienced reality, in taking theological reflection into the lives of real people with real spiritual quests and challenges. I also write because "birds sing." To paraphrase Eric Liddell of the film "Chariots of Fire,"

> God gave me a writer's spirit and a theologian's mind
> and when I write, I can feel God's pleasure!

God uses the materials of the world, the alphabet of creation, the hues of the cosmos, to redeem, heal, and create. God takes the beauty and wreckage of life – life God has previously influenced and then given to the universe for its creative contribution – saves it everlastingly in God's own experience, redeems and transforms it, and then releases back into the world to inspire further creaturely creativity. The Artist of the Universe and the Poet of the World, God's presence in the world inspires our quest to leave a mark, to make a difference, to make our lives a work of art and do something beautiful for God. As poet Lawrence Ferlinghetti affirms: "Every great poem fulfills a longing and puts life back together." The joining of divine and human poetry heals the broken spirit and provides meaning and fulfillment to an everchanging world.

Every artist, even my grandchildren drawing with pencil and paper, creating paper mache figures, or painting on canvas, has a vision. And God has a vision, too. God's vision is guided by the inspiration of truth, beauty, and goodness. While these terms are abstract, I believe Whitehead means something like Jeremiah 29:11, spoken in a time of national crisis:

For surely I know the plans I have for you, says the Lord, plans for your welfare and not for harm, to give you a future with hope.

Or perhaps, the meaning is found in one of my favorite Christmas carols which defines God's rule as love, truth, grace, and justice, and not control or domination.

[God] rules the world with truth and grace,
And makes the nations prove
The glories of His righteousness,
And wonders of His love,
And wonders of His love,
And wonders, wonders, of His love.

The ultimate pragmatist and relativist, the inventive artist and architect, the Most Moved Mover, is also the ultimate visionary, imaging galaxies and spinning them into existence. Visualizing a child's future and providing possibilities and energy for significant adults and child alike. Envisioning Shalom and then inspiring prophets, protesters, prayers, and protectors to work toward embodying God's realm "on earth as well as heaven."

Through the wilderness of pandemic, systemic injustice, climate change, incivility, and apathy, God leads us with a vision. Pointing us toward the far horizon and challenging us to keep our eyes on the prize – the day of justice and reconciliation, of healing and peace.

Sharing in Divine Artistry. This spiritual exercise is twofold. The first aspect is to pause and notice: this time notice and appreciate the wonders of divine artistry. In "The Summer Day," Cape Cod poet Mary Oliver describes the amazing complexity of a grasshopper. In *The Pilgrim at Tinker's Creek,* Annie Dillard is transfixed by light shining through the trees, bringing forth the holy light of all things. Gerard Manley Hopkins praises God in the "pied beauty" of brinded cows, finch's wings, and chestnuts. Walt Whitman describes the wondrous beauty of trades people and swimmers on a summer day and avers that all is miracle. Louis

Armstrong proclaims with gratitude, "It's a wonderful world." Let your senses roam in wonder and radical amazement as you give thanks for this good Earth.

In the second exercise, explore your own artistry and creativity. God's creative wisdom flows through you, inspiring you to be a poet and artist. Take time to explore your "inner" poet, artist, and woodworker – or whatever media you choose. Simply enjoy the process with no concern for the product. Rejoice in bringing something into the world that is novel in its expression of your gifts, whether in words, colors, dance steps, song, hammer and saw, trowel and seed.

19.

*For the kingdom of heaven is with us today. The action of the
fourth phase is the love of God for the world. It is the particular
providence for particular occasions. What is done in the world is
transformed into a reality in heaven, and the reality in heaven
passes back into the world...the love in the world passes into the
love in heaven, and floods back into the world. God is the great
companion – the fellow sufferer who understands...In this way,
the insistent craving that zest for existence be refreshed by the
everpresent, unfading importance of our actions, which perish and
yet live forevermore.*[49]

God and the world exist in a symbiotic relationship. In the
ongoing Creative Processes of the Universe, there has never been a
world without God, or a God without the world. In the ongoing
adventure of Divine Creativity, God is constantly calling forth
possibilities and the universe is constantly responding. God has
always created, whether in our universe, or in its predecessors, inspired by God's vision of the Beauty that is and can become. In the
universe and human life, God's love flows into the world in terms
of vision, providential encounters, inspiration, the emergence of
thin places, and persons chosen to share more fully God's vision
with humankind. The world flows into God, shaping the quality of
God's experience, giving God materials with which to create, and
inspiring divine artistry, lament, creativity, and challenge. And then
God's love flows back into the world with creative and redemptive
possibilities.

God is the great companion, calling and responding, rejoicing
with every achievement, elated with the return of the wayward,
delighting in the breach of a Right Whale off Cape Cod's coast,
frolicking with a child at play, fluttering with a grasshopper on a
summer day, exhilarated by Serena Williams' serving at Wimbledon
and equally delighted with a sprinter at a Special Olympics event.
God is the ultimate pleasure seeker and joy receiver.

---

49 Ibid., 351.

God is the ultimate empath. God is the fellow sufferer who understands. God feels our pain and grief. Our sense of abandonment and guilt. Our loneliness and pain. God comforts an elder dying of COVID, unable to say "goodbye" to their children and God mourns with the children, unable to sit at the bedside. God moves through the interstices of dementia patients and the loneliness of their spouses. Even when we plunge ourselves in darkness through substance use, depression, and misconduct, believing no one will accept us and that we deserve no acceptance, God reveals light in darkness and guideposts when we are lost.

Only a suffering God can save, so says Dietrich Bonhoeffer awaiting judgment, and eventual execution, by the Nazi tribunal. There is a cross at the heart of God. Calvary does not supernaturally change God's relationship to the world. The Cross on Calvary reveals God's everlasting and ubiquitous immersion in the pain and suffering of the world, the depth of divine embeddedness in our pain and violence. Long before Whitehead, the Hebraic prophet Hosea captured the spirit of God's relational love:

> Yet it was I who taught Ephraim to walk,
>   I took them up in my arms;
>   but they did not know that I healed them.
> I led them with cords of human kindness,
>   with bands of love.
> I was to them like those
>   who lift infants to their cheeks.
>   I bent down to them and fed them. (Hosea 11:3-4)

The One Who Celebrates and Suffers also Harvests and Plants. The immediate moment perishes, but that moment of joy and suffering is forever imprinted in God, the marks of the nails remain, just as the sound of laughter endures. Nothing is lost in God. No struggle or achievement forgotten. No life marginalized or silenced. Whatever is loved endures forever.

Sharing God's Empathy. Spiritual growth emerges from the movement from apathy to empathy. From emotional distance to intimate identification. To feel the feelings of others from the perspective of your experience. Spiritual growth involves opening to the pain and beauty, the suffering and joy, of the world. It is a widening of emotional connection to embrace others' feelings without losing your personal center or shutting down from defensiveness.

In the spirit of the Ultimate Empath open your experience to the experiences of others. Look beyond their words to glimpse feeling tones. Listen for joy and pain, and excitement and boredom. Listen to your own feelings. Let your news feed or televised news open your heart to others, even those with whom you disagree. Look more deeply than their words into their heart, and let your empathy guide you toward creative responses, whether to families economically suffering from the pandemic, children still separated from their parents on the USA borderlands, immigrants fleeing dangerous gangs and repressive regimes in Central American, persons looking for work, siblings grieving the loss of a family member from COVID. Let your empathy be a call to prayer, communion, and response to help heal the world.

The prayers you make with the world and God may lead you to lamentation for the suffering of the world personally and globally. You may lament hardheartedness in a time of pandemic. The death toll, not numbers but real beating and loving heart persons. You may lament the foolishness of politicians who promote dishonesty and division when national unity is need. Your lamentation may lead you to reach out to grieving persons and advocating – even protesting – public policies built on power without presence and control without compassion.

20.

There stands an inexorable law that apart from some tran-
scendent aim the civilized life either wallows in pleasure or relapses
slowly into a barren repetition with waning intensities of feeling.[50]

Whitehead sees the progress of history and civilization as an adventure of ideas in which great ideas and novel possibilities propel our lives and civilizations forward toward new horizons. The lure of adventure calls us forward beyond current achievements toward new frontiers in art, science, literature, and morality. Progress in civilization weds idealism with political progress, expanding the scope of rights and statecraft toward wider and wider circles of inclusion. Whereas once ethical consideration was accorded only to privileged groups (for example, males, European Americans, the economic majority) now the full range of human experience is honored and deserving of ethical affirmation, with the possibility of enlarging this circle to embrace the non-human world.

Whether in religion, society, or politics, transcendental aims are both alluring and frightening. We feel the energy of possibility and the vitality of change. Without change, civilization and religion stagnate. Christianity must change or die, chants John Shelby Spong. American flourishing requires letting go of past achievements and power centers. New voices are welcomed and novel realities imagined. Homogeneity gives way to diversity. Tradition gives way to novelty.

As exciting and necessary as transcendent visions are for civilization, politics, and religion, there is a danger for civilizations and political systems as well as faith traditions to experience these life-giving changes solely as threatening. Old certainties and privileges are put at risk raising the level of anxiety and reaction. Racial and religious dominance collapses under the weight of wider vistas of inclusion and affirmation. Changes in demographics lead to reactionary behaviors in response. Change is seen as an attack on

---

50 Alfred North Whitehead, *Adventures of Ideas* (New York: Free Press, 1933, 1967), 85.

our deepest values. In the United States, the transcendent vision that led to the election of an African American president, women's rights, ethnic diversity, and marriage equality led to an equally powerful backlash, embodied in the rise of overt racism, hate crimes toward the LGBTQ community, and attacks on immigrants. Many Conservative Christians see any growth in human rights as an attack on their faith, once and for all delivered to the saints and dictated by inerrant scriptures, fixating on wedding cakes while denying climate change and the traumatic separation of children from their parents on the USA borderlands. At such times, persons of faith and patrons of democracy would do well to remember Whitehead's assertion that the pure and inflexible conservative goes against the nature of the universe.

The wisdom of the American vision, at its best, is the quest for "a more perfect union." The vision of "liberty and justice for all" flickers throughout history, challenged by champions of sexual, gender, and racial exceptionalism. The ideal of "life, liberty, and the pursuit of happiness," regardless of race, gender, sexuality, nation of origin, ethnicity, and religion unsettles those wedded to privilege. Yet the unsettling, despite our fears, may be God's vision embodied in the quest for change.

Personal, civilizational, and political transcendence requires letting go of the familiar and going beyond racial, religious, and economic self-interest and privilege and nation-first ideologies to imagine and then embody larger circles of justice and wellbeing. This is "the zest of self-forgetful transcendence belonging to Civilization at its height," according to Whitehead.[51] The sacrifice demanded by a transcendent vision gives birth to civilizational, religious, and political vitality and energizes the ongoing quest for the more perfect union and a sustainable planet.

The Quest for a Transcendent Vision. God seeks to give us more than we can ask or imagine. God shatters our familiarities with calls to adventure, personally and politically. The reality of God's transcendent vision, coming to us as provocative possibilities for

51 Ibid., 295.

persons, nations, and the planet, invites us to examine the contrast between the status quo and the open horizon of divine possibility.

In a time of prayerfulness, reflect on your life. Toward what new possibilities is God calling to you? Toward what creative contrast between past and future is God luring you? What new thing will expand and deepen your life? What first steps are you invited to take to open to God's dream for you?

Continue your prayerfulness as you reflect on God's transcendent vision for your nation. Toward what new possibilities is God calling your nation? What past limitations and injustices need to be challenged in light of God's vision? Where does the soul of the nation need healing to be faithful to God's vision? As a citizen, what first steps are you invited to take to help move forward the arc of justice in your nation? Beyond that, toward what creative vision is God calling you as a planetary citizen and to the nations of the world as partners in healing the world?

21.

The Discord of the Universe arises from the fact that modes of Beauty are various, and not of necessity compatible. And yet some admixture of Discord is a necessary factor in the transition from mode to mode. The objective life of the past and the future in the present is an inevitable element of disturbance. Discord may take the form of freshness or hope, or it may be horror or pain.[52]

Peace is the harmony of harmonies, healing tragedy through the experience of Beauty and Meaning. Yet, the way to global consciousness, the path to world loyalty, often involves discord and disagreement. The moral and spiritual arcs move toward open horizons. The quest for justice challenges the status quo, and that can be painful and conflictual as well as exhilarating and exciting.

Life flows and evolves. New eras call for new duties. Evolution involves the evocation of intensity, variety, and complexity of experience and impact, and the mere fact of forward movement creates discord. Species complement each other in the ecological niches; they also conflict with one another in the quest for dominance and survival. Creativity and growth involve the right blend of order and chaos, predictability and novelty. Life itself is robbery, Whitehead observes, but the pillage among higher organisms must be justified by a greater good.

Discord is at the heart of the spiritual adventure and quest for justice. Consider Amos challenging the wealthy and powerful:

I hate, I despise your festivals,
    and I take no delight in your solemn assemblies.
Take away from me the noise of your songs;
 I will not listen to the melody of your harps.
But let justice roll down like waters,
 and righteousness like an ever-flowing stream.
(Amos 5:21, 23-24)

---

52 Ibid., 266.

Imagine how threatening Amos' words must have seemed to economic, religious, and political communities intent on preserving power and privilege. Progress in history involves the clash of visions of reality, conflict between the ideal and actual. In our time, we can imagine the discord created by Mahatma Gandhi and Martin Luther King; the conflict provoked by Rosa Parks and John Lewis. Even a little child, like Ruby Bridges, entering a white elementary school, or teenage Greta Thunberg, confronting global climate change on behalf of future generations, challenge established understandings of race and economics. Stonewall and Black Lives Matter remind us that the national patient is diseased, and political and ethical surgery is needed. Discord is painful but necessary in personal, political, and planetary progress and evolution. What appears to be chaotic and disorderly may be the birth pangs of a new age.

The prophet imagines a new heaven and new earth that puts to risk old familiarities and power structures. Socrates challenges the elite and powerful and is condemned to death. Jesus turns over the tables in the Jerusalem Temple, and eventually must travel the way of the Cross. The prophetic imagination, as Old Testament scholar and theologian Walter Brueggemann asserts, presents an alternative and painful alternative to the injustice of the status quo.

Although we often identify God's impact on our lives as comforting and calming, God also agitates those who are the comfortable with economic injustice, nationalism, war making, and racial privilege. As the organ of novelty, God's vision often creates discord between established truths and social patterns and the far vistas of human wholeness. The adventures of ideas are exciting and inspiring. They are also unsettling. Even the reformer and protester may find themselves unsettled when other prophets challenge them to exceed their current understandings of justice, economics, and race.

Discord is interpersonal, social, political, and metaphysical. Whitehead notes that growth always pushes us beyond our personal and political comfort zones.

Given the vigor of adventure, sooner or later the leap of imagination reaches beyond the safe limits of the epoch…it then produces the dislocations and confusions marking the advent of the new ideals of civilized effort…a real contrast between what has been and what may be…the vigor of adventure beyond the safeties of the past. Without adventure civilization is in decay.[53]

Discord is grounded in interplay of actual and ideal, tradition and novelty. Variety and pluralism lead to contrast. Change leads to challenging the past. Growth requires jettison past enjoyments. Our task is to provoke healthy and life-supportive discord. Discord grounded in the vision of the Peace that passes understanding and Achievement beyond our self-interest. Whitehead would applaud the counsel of John Lewis, recalling in 2020 the carnage at Edmund Pettus Bridge on the Bloody Sunday, March 7, 1965, "Get into good trouble, necessary trouble, to redeem the soul of America." Yet, out of the discord of justice seeking that provoked state-sponsored violence, transformation emerged. In the pain of protest, the seeds of hope and change were sowed and the United States took baby steps toward the Civil and Voting Rights Acts and the election of President Barack Obama and Vice President Kamala Harris. We have a long way to go in the adventure of USA history toward that "more perfect union" and there will be discord on the way. But beyond discord is the dream of Promised Land and the realization of Tragic Beauty.

Embracing Discord. This section's spiritual practice invites you to a personal and political life review regarding the role of discord. Where have you experienced the positive value of discord? What old familiarities gave way to embrace new possibilities? What were the gains that occurred due to your opening to discord as a catalyst for change? Where are you experiencing discord today?

As you look at our national or planetary situation, where do you see discordant experiences? Do you see movements toward justice and healing in these discordant situations? What old fa-

---

53 Ibid., 279.

100 A Month of Meditations for Process-Relational Pilgrims

miliarities are being challenged? Do you see the presence of God in these situations of discord? What hopes do you have for the outcome of these discordant experiences? How can you further the creative discord necessary for social transformation?

22.

The teleology of the universe is aimed at the production of beauty.[54]

We live in a lively, evolving, value-laden universe, grounded in the Creative Wisdom and Loving Artistry of God. The heavens declare the glory of God and so do our cells and circulatory system. In this time of pandemic, we rejoice in the intelligent beauty of the immune and lymphatic systems, identifying, capturing, and flushing it out of our bodies. We delight in the ability of vaccines to marshal our immune system in response to COVID.

According to process-relational theologian Patricia Adams Farmer, the quest for beauty is at the heart of the evolutionary process. God evokes beauty over billions of years, emerging in our current universe from the Big Bang or Big Birth, moving from simplicity to complexity and unconscious to conscious experience, and instinct to wise intentionality.

> Beauty, at its most divine, integrates both elements [harmony and intensity] into a larger frame: that is, Beauty as *intense harmony* is a celebration of contrasts within a larger, harmonious whole. Beauty, then, is the very yearning of God for our evolving world–a world of creative movement, where the diverse elements strive not toward bland sameness, but rather toward rich and complex forms of well-being.[55]

The organ of novelty is also the inspiration of beauty, the beauty of the universe in its totality and its various parts, and the beauty of experience, our own enjoyment of beauty. The Genesis creation stories proclaim the "goodness" of life, apart from human interest. Long before human sin entered the world, God birthed an original wholeness, reflected in God's ever-present lure for joy, creativity,

---

54 Ibid., 265.
55 Patricia Adams Farmer, *Beauty and Process Theology* (Gonzalez, FL: Energion Publications, 2020, 5.

complexity, and intensity of experience. Psalm 148 captures the world of praise, parented forth by God's Loving and Creative Wisdom. Within this doxological universe, human life finds meaning and inspiration.

> Praise the LORD!
> Praise the LORD from the heavens;
>   praise him in the heights!
> Praise him, all his angels;
>   praise him, all his host!
>
> Praise him, sun and moon;
>   praise him, all you shining stars!
> Praise him, you highest heavens,
>   and you waters above the heavens!
>
> Praise the LORD from the earth,
>   you sea monsters and all deeps,
> fire and hail, snow and frost,
>   stormy wind fulfilling his command!
>
> Mountains and all hills,
>   fruit trees and all cedars!
> Wild animals and all cattle,
>   creeping things and flying birds! (Psalm 148:1-4, 7-10)

The Psalms conclude with the affirmation that the breath of God flowing through all life gives life, joy, and meaning to all creation, "let everything that breathes, praise God." (Psalm 150:6) A bumper sticker I see each summer as I walk on Craigville Beach counsels, "Keep Sublime Alive," reminding me with Dostoevsky that the world is saved by beauty. As God's companions in beautifying the world, we are challenged both to see beauty and be beauty and commit, along with Mother Teresa, to doing something beautiful for God. Then, our days will be full of wonder and inspiration, discerning with each step the wisdom of the Navajo spirit guides, "with beauty all around me, I walk."

Being a Beauty Maker. We can see beauty and we can add beauty. With the Navajo spirit guide, we can walk with beauty all around us. We can look for beauty wherever we are, in human and non-human life, in the heavens above and the movements of our souls. The perception of beauty inspires reverence and gratitude. The perception of beauty inspires agency and artistry. We can choose to do something beautiful for God, as Mother (Saint) Teresa counsels. Our lives can be dedicated to beauty and in so doing we contribute to the arc of beauty flowing through our lives and the universe. Beauty involves adding harmony and intensity and making room for creativity in the lives around us.

In our personal lives, we can prayerfully ask throughout the day, "How can I bring beauty to this situation? How can my action here bring greater beauty to those around me?" In my life as a citizen, I can advocate for a politics of beauty. I can work for public policy, environmental initiatives, and economic practices that create an infrastructure of beauty. That enables people to have sufficient wellbeing to focus on beauty of experience and creativity. We can promote governmental policies that, in Whitehead's words, enable people first to live, and then live well and better.

23.

The good of the Universe cannot lie in indefinite postpone-
ment. The day of Day of Judgment is an important notion: but
the Day is always with us... The effect of the present on the future
is the business of morals...Morals consist in the aim at the ideal,
and at its lowest the prevention of relapse to lower levels. Thus
stagnation is the deadly foe of morality.[56]

Each morning I awaken with the words, "this is the day that
God has made and I will rejoice and be glad in it." These words
remind to orient my attitudes toward wonder, appreciation, gratitude, and agency. "This is the day." Now is the only time there is!
Grounded in the past and leaning toward the future, this day, this
moment, is a "thin place" where heaven and earth, infinity and finitude meet, to create this Holy Here and Now. This is the moment
of decision. The embrace of divine possibilities and the cutting off
other possibilities. The world lives by its incarnation of God and
the whole universe conspires to create this moment of experience.

Perhaps few philosophers prized the interplay of the temporal
and eternal, concrete and abstract, and infinite and finite than
Whitehead. Still, Whitehead was well-aware that the process is the
reality and that the impact of past and future meet in the self-creation of this moment of experience. God's realm is not abstract,
it exists on earth. God's dream remains ineffectual on this planet
until we embrace and embody it. God cannot achieve God's vision
without human partnership. This is the moment of decision. In this
concrete moment, we align ourselves with the moral and spiritual
arcs of history, moving from self-interest to world loyalty, or turn
toward self-interest and planetary chaos.

Whitehead joins metaphysics, axiology (the theory of value),
and ethics in proclaiming the significance of concrete Here and
Now experience. The future is open. The omega point, the vision
of Shalom, is being created by what happens in the ongoing process

---

56 Ibid., 269.

of individual self-creation, community policies, and international priorities.

I have long prized the words of Rabbi Hillel the Great (110 BCE-10 CE) as wise counsel for process-relational thinkers:

If I am not for myself, who will be for me?
If I am not for others, what am I?
And if not now, when?

Self-affirmation and self-creation are at the heart of life. I am the artist of my experience, joining the impact of the past and the lure of the future in a moment of creative synthesis and transformation. My self-creation is my gift to the world. My agency shapes life beyond me. As I love myself, aiming for wholeness and fulfillment, living out God's possibilities in my unique way, I contribute to my future and to the future of the world around me. This is the moment to keep my eyes on the prize of greatness of experience, of growing in wisdom and stature.

Now is the day of salvation! Or, as Whitehead asserts, "the Day of Judgement Judgment is always with us." Martin Luther King pens *Why We Can't Wait* as a clarion call to social justice not just for African Americans but for healing the soul of America. Greta Thunberg challenges political leaders and baby boomers to be "good ancestors," to recognize that the clock is ticking in terms of the irreversible impact of global climate change and the importance of action NOW. When George Floyd, a victim of systemic racism, cries out "I can't breathe," he is calling the nation to get out the crash carts and administer spiritual and political CPR to save its soul. We are part of a grand cosmic journey. We are children of the Infinity of time and space, and yet infinity is lived out in this moment. If God is the circle whose center is everywhere and whose circumference is nowhere, then we are responsible for our personal center in this Holy Here and Now and its impact on every future center.

In this moment, this day of decision, will we advance God's aim at Shalom and Beauty or will we embrace the downward forces of greed, consumption, racial superiority, and nationalism? We are the creators of the future, contributing either ugliness or beauty to God and the world by our choices today.

The Spirit of Now. Now is the only moment there is! Our decisions occur moment by moment and shape the long haul of our lives and the world. While some issues can wait, there are other issues that cry out, "If not now, when?" We can ask ourselves, "it not now for _____, when?" How would you fill in this blank to respond to the world's needs, to have alignment with God's aim at beauty? To be in synch with the moral and spiritual arcs of the universe? As I ponder this question based on process-relational theological insights, I ask:

- If not now, when - in responding to climate change?
- If not now, when - in preserving the wellsprings of democracy?
- If not now, when - in ensuring every child can have health care, safe housing, and quality education?
- If not now, when - in responding to global – and national – food insecurity and malnutrition?
- If not now, when - in seeking liberty and justice for all?
- If not now, when in - responding to gun violence in the USA?

We may have similar "day of judgment" issues in our personal and professional lives. What is important is the recognition that in a world of process, we can't forever do what is right for ourselves and others. This is the moment and day of salvation!

24.

*Peace is the removal of inhibition and not its introduction.
It results in a wider sweep of conscious interest. It enlarges the field
of attention. Thus peace is self-control at its widest, - at the width
where the 'self' has been lost, and interest has been transferred
to coordinations wider than personality…Peace is so essential to
civilization. It is the barrier   against narrowness…the love of
[humankind] as such.[57]*

The great religions of the world promise peace in the challenges of life. In a time of national crisis, the Psalmist counsels "be still and know that I am God" and proclaims God's unswerving faithfulness in the maelstrom of history. (Psalm 46:10) Gautama Buddha faced temptation under the Bo Tree, grounded in his recognition that equanimity comes from embracing change without attachment or possessiveness. In the wake of the cross and resurrection, the Risen Jesus breathed on his followers and promised, the peace that comes from God's Spirit animating and inspiring their lives. (John 20:21-22)

Peace is a spiritual and theological virtue, the gift of vision, perspective, and largeness of spirit. Whitehead's vision of peace reflects his understanding of God. Some peoples' gods are brittle and exclusive, separating the world in categories of saved and unsaved and friend and foe, stingy with both revelation and blessing. Those who follow such images of God see truth and power as limited. Any admission of theological, ethical, or political fallibility or limitation threatens the entire edifice of faith, whether it involves the relationship of scripture and science, the possibility of truth and salvation in other religions, or questioning conspiracy theories.

In contrast, Whitehead proclaims a universal, large-spirited God, similar in spirit to the image of divinity described by Plato, the philosopher Whitehead most admires. In connecting cosmology and spirituality, Plato asserted that the Creator is "good, and in him that is good no envy arises ever concerning anything; and be-

---

57 Ibid., 285-286.

ing devoid of envy He desired that all should be, so far as possible, like unto divinity." (29e) Those who follow God's way, creatively patterning their lives after God's creative wisdom, thinking divine thoughts "will so far as it is possible for human nature to partake of immortality" in the world of change as well as in eternity. (90d)

Following Plato, Whitehead describes God in terms of goodness, beauty, creativity, and possibility. God is all-embracing and all loving, even as God's vision is aimed at the production of beauty in unique moments of experience. A large-spirited God inspires large-spirited religion. In contrast, small-spirited gods inspire small-spirited, divisive, and vengeful religions.

The God of Peace embraces both restlessness and equanimity. God's quest for intensity and breadth of experience reveals a divine passion for liveliness and growth. God's work is always in process, never complete, and propelling us toward the far horizons of planetary and personal healing. The prophetic quest, inspired by the encounter with God, challenges the injustice of the current status quo – and every age's status quo - in relation to God's vision of Shalom. God feels the pain of the marginalized, oppressed, and impoverished, and in drawing close to God, the prophet experiences the divine empathy and passion for social transformation. Jesus challenges dead ritual, weeps over Jerusalem, and disrupts commerce in the Jerusalem Temple, inspired by his experience and embodiment of the divine passion for Shalom.

Spiritual passion takes us beyond self-interest to compassionate world loyalty. The fragile, self-interested self is always at risk. Focusing on prosperity and personal success narrow our field of interest. We cling to the individualistic, independent self, unable to empathize or promote the wellbeing of others. Their gain is our loss, whether it involves relationships, economics, racial privilege, political power, or national sovereignty. The small-spirited person gains the world, reaching the heights of political power and economic largesse, but in process experience the loss of their soul, the wellsprings of empathy, compassion, and companionship.

In contrast, Jesus once said that those who lose their lives will find them. Those who sacrifice individual self-interest will gain a world of companions and friends and will be at home everywhere. The peaceful self may even sacrifice enlightenment and life itself, characteristic of the Bodhisattva and the Dying-Rising Jesus, to bring healing and wholeness to our world of pain. The strange irony of embodying the mind of Christ, described by the Apostle Paul in Philippians 2:5-11) is that by letting go our world expands and we experience the harmony of harmonies that characterizes peace and equanimity – the peace that passes understanding – bringing comfort and healing that soothes the troubled souls of individuals and nations.

Having the Spacious Mind of Christ. To illuminate this passage, we will explore Philippians 2:5-11 through the process of *lectio divina*, or "holy reading," taught by Benedict of Nursia (480-547 CE) and his followers. A process-relational approach to *lectio divina* follows these steps:

1. A time of stillness.
2. Prayer for gratitude.
3. Read a scripture or other inspiring reading slowly and meditatively twice.
4. Listen for the emotional tone of the reading.
5. Discern a word, image, musical piece emerging from the reading.
6. Let the word roll around your mind, leading to experiencing other words or images.
7. Let the word or image soak in by focusing on it, perhaps repeating or connecting it with other words or images.
8. Ask the relationship of the word, image, tune to your life and the world.
9. Ask how you would change if you took the word seriously in your life.
10. Ask for God's guidance in embodying the word.
11. Conclude with gratitude for God's inspiration.

Take time to live with Philippians 2:5-11, reading and praying it, letting your imagination expand with words and images, discerning how living with this scripture might change your life.

25.

*At the heart of the nature of things, there are always the
dream of youth and the harvest of tragedy. The Adventure of the
Universe starts with the dream and reaps Tragic Beauty. This is the
secret of the union of Zest with Peace: - That the suffering attains
its end in a Harmony of Harmonies. The immediate experience of
this Final Fact, with its union of Youth and Tragedy, is the sense
of Peace. In this way the world receives its persuasion toward such
perfections as are possible for its diverse individual occasions.*[58]

God has a dream and so do we. The Adventure of the Universe, the infinite wellspring of possibility, inspires the birth of
each moment's experience. Our own dreams shape our immediate experiences and long hopes. Without a dream, life languishes.
We become content with the status quo in our own lives and our
national agenda. Zest for life emerges when each moment's possibilities inspire and energize. We awaken each morning looking
forward to the day ahead. We relish the excitement change brings
into our lives.

As I look at young children, they are all possibility. As I look
at the passions of youth – for love, social transformation, planetary
change – I am filled with gratitude and concern. I see the energy
of the youth protesting gun violence, confronting climate change,
volunteering at soup kitchens, and building homes for Habitat
for Humanity. I see the joy of youth exploring new adventures in
self-discovery and falling in love. Their passion reminds me of my
own youthful passion and idealism. I also remember the poignancy
of disappointment, broken hearts, failure, and the dashing of hopes
from childhood and youth to age. I remember and still wince when
I see the adult pushback of youthful idealism, whether the Parkland
youth or Greta Thunberg, dismissing their concerns. I yearn for
the experience of Tragic Beauty. I know we are saved by Beauty,
joined with the wisdom of the age and passion for transformation.

58 Ibid., 296.

Hope and zest depend on a sense of Peace, a trust that our lives matter and that even our failures are a pathway to future personal and communal adventures. Youthful passion lives in the present moment and sometimes lacks the perspective that age brings. With age comes patience, but age must not lose the passion for the ideal, for the dream, for novel possibilities that inspire novel behaviors. Like the child and youth, we also need to know that our lives matter and that they are treasured in the nature of things. That the quest for justice, even if it is deferred, changes the world in ways the passage of time cannot erase.

God is the Great Adventurer. God is the Ultimate Recipient of Experience, receiving the gifts of our lives and treasuring them eternally in God's ever-evolving memory and interactions with the world. In that marriage of actuality and idealism, tradition and adventure, and death and immorality, we find hope in the Great Adventure of God. Hope described in dream and poetry, in the wisdom of the Artist of the World, described by Patricia Adams Farmer.

> Re-write our tragedies into the larger
> sea of innumerable imaginings.
> Feed our follies to creatures without violence,
> by the persuasion of your pen: new words
> strung together into rare pink pearls
> awaiting discovery by divers who love the sea.[59]

The world is saved by beauty, tragic beauty that gives meaning to our perpetually perishing, always adventuring, life on our swiftly-turning planet.

A Spirituality of Tragic Beauty. Another traditional spiritual practice congruent with process-relational is the Examen, pioneered by Ignatius of Loyola, parent of the Jesuit tradition. In Examen, you look back on the day, or a period of your life, opening to the God-moments as well as times you felt distant from God. In

---

59 Patricia Adams Farmer, *The Metaphor Maker (Create Space, 2009)*, 350.

praying the seasons of your life, you can identify and enhance the presence of God in your life.

In this practice set aside at least half an hour, or a series of days, to reflect on God's presence in the tragedy as well as beauty of your life through the following process:

1. Stillness and prayer of gratitude for God's presence in your life.
2. Look back at your life story, identifying moments of beauty in your life.
3. Continue looking back, identifying moments of tragedy.
4. Ask, where was God present in these moments? What helped you make it through? What did you learn?
5. Experience the sense and intricate interdependence of tragedy and beauty in your life.
6. Where does your experience of tragic beauty open to future movements of God's presence in your life?
7. Give thanks for your future with God, growing in companionship with God in healing the world.

26.

*Morality consists in the control of the process to maximize
importance. It is the aim at greatness of experience in the various
dimensions belonging to it... Morality is always the aim at the
union of harmony, intensity, and vividness which involves the
perfection of importance for that occasion.*[60]

Value and importance are at the heart of Whitehead's cosmology and process-relational theology. "Value" relates to the uniqueness of every moment of experience. Every moment of experience, whether human or non-human, angelic or cellular, is a center of value, a creative synthesis of the universe from its perspective. To exist is to experience, and to experience is for a creature, a moment in time, to have value for itself, apart from any benefit to others. Whatever exists matters, and is loved by God, even if it is at cross purposes with human interests. The majestic conclusion to the Book of Job speaks of God's creativity at work in the experiences of leviathan, behemoth, ostrich, mountain goat, and horse. They are wild, unpredictable, and yet God delights in them. The Psalmist describes a universe of praise in which snow, wind, hail, sea monster, earth and air creatures, praise God along with humankind. Whatever can praise deserves moral consideration. The process is the reality, and the reality is value laden.

"Importance" describes the quest for greater intensity, complexity, beauty, and harmony of experience. Importance is concerned with realizing the highest values and possibilities for any given moment – a child imagining they are a superhero, a teen experiencing first love, a young adult discerning their vocation, an elder on a vision quest to face mortality with grace and the desire to be a "good ancestor" to future generations. Importance is fullness and beauty of experience, exploration and desire for wholeness, adventure and the redemption of suffering and failure. Importance

---

60 Alfred North Whitehead, *Modes of Thought* (New York: Free Press, 1968), 13-14. [1938]

involves being able to be agents of our destiny as unique reflections of God's loving creativity.

Metaphysics inspires morality and contemplation awakens compassion. The world is healed one moment at a time, the world evolves toward Shalom one moment at a time, even though the path forward is fragile and tentative. Morality aims at promoting beauty of experience in the now and the future and takes us beyond human experience to the experiences of non-humans as well as God. My Golden Doodle Tucker's joy when I take him to run on the beach reflects and contributes to God's joy in the creative process. My affirmation of my grandchildren's "make believe" games helps grow their spirits and brings joy to the Parent of all creativity. "Make believe" can be morally and spiritually valuable as a source of provocative possibilities whether you are a poet or inventor. Our imaginations connect us to a Deeper Imagination from whom creative possibilities emerge and inject new possibilities into the world. Without "make believe," the entertaining of currently "unrealistic" ideals, the world is doomed to stagnation and repetition. Without the vivid counterfactual imagination, slaves will not be freed, women will not achieve equality, marginalized persons will not see themselves as God's children, and members of the LGBTQ community will not see holiness when they look in the mirror. Without "make believe" entertaining of future visions, we will not pursue new ways of behaving, explore new avenues of vocation, or let go of the familiar past to embody larger visions of self and social responsibility.

Morality does not require belief in God. It does depend on greater visions of ourselves and the world, and trust that our actions matter in creating the future. Morality involves at its depths an implicit congruence, recognized or not, with higher values, described by persons of faith as God's presence and aim at intensity and complexity for the moment and the future. Our partnership, known or unknown, with God furthers the moral arc of history by bringing wholeness to the world one experience at a time.

Behold, wherever you are, that you are on holy ground. Jacob awakens from a dream of a ladder of angels and exclaims, "God was in this place – and I did not know it." Jacob realizes first that Beth-El is the gateway to heaven and then every place is a gateway to heaven, a "thin place," where divinity is revealed in life's perpetual perishing. Behold, every encounter is holy. Behold, every creature is holy. Reverence for life is demanded, even when we must alter or take certain lives for survival or challenge injustice and mean spiritedness in interpersonal and political relationships.

Taking seriously the importance of life, the value-laden nature of reality, means that our prophetic protest aims at healing the soul of oppressor and oppressed alike. That we confront the destructive powers of the world with the life-transforming power of love, and seek reconciliation in the chaos of political decision-making, the quest for healthy relationships, and creating structures of community order and national security.

Inspired by the metaphysical and theological vision of universal value, we seek a realm of concrete self-realization amid the conflict and chaos of life, knowing that we are not alone in our quest. We are companioned by a Love, Power, Justice, and Wisdom Greater than Our Own, who inspires and cherishes are efforts to heal the world.

Spirituality of Nurturing Importance of Experience. In process-relational thought, experience matters. Authentic, innocent, and life-supportive happiness matters. We are challenged to maximize importance, fullness of experience, in the present moment and over the long haul. Bringing joy to my ninety-pound Golden Doodle by taking him to gallop on the beach adds to the joy of life as a whole. God feels a dog's joy at running along the beach. Reading with my grands adds to the joy of the universe and grows their spirits. Tutoring a child at school opens new horizons and adds to the zest of the moment. Standing for justice saves lives and creates an environment where parents and children can experience safety as a prerequisite for happiness and growth. Joy is not self-interested:

the joy we feel when we join our wellbeing with others heals the world one moment at a time.

Today, make a commitment to maximize importance. To maximize joy. Make a commitment to look toward the greater happiness in every encounter. Even in conflict situations look beyond self-interest to resolutions that will add to the beauty to the world. Experience your authentic relational joy as reflecting God's joy and contributing to the joy of the world and the Ultimate Recipient of Value. Take a moment and reflect on the contagious, world saving joy you can add by:

- Being attentive to your spouse, partner, or close friend.
- Doing something for the pure innocent pleasure of it.
- Spending time with a child, grandchild, or young person – playing, reading, coaching, tutoring, listening.
- Making music, drawing, reading, writing, singing.
- Creating pleasurable moments for human and non-human companions.
- Advocating for a politics of joy – aiming to nurture the pursuit of authentic, healthy happiness – through public policy.
- Delighting in group activities such as worship, classes, games, parties.

As one of my process-relational mentors David Ray Griffin asserted, "God wants you to enjoy. God wants all of us to enjoy." When we live joyfully, we can feel God's pleasure and add to the pleasure of others.

27.

In fact, the world beyond is so intimately entwined in our own natures that unconsciously we identify our more vivid experiences of it with ourselves...but the body is part of the external world, continuous with it. In which it is just as much a part of nature as anything else there – a river, or a mountain, or a cloud. Also, if we are fussily exact, we cannot define where a body begins and where external nature ends...the human body is that region of the world which is the primary field of human expressions.[61]

I recalll many mornings when I meandered across the beaches of Centerville, Massachusetts, where I lived. I walked as the Buddhists say between rain drops as I was buffeted by gusty northeastern winds. I felt the sting of rain drops on my cheeks and moisture on my tennis shoes. I also felt the joy of movement, the ease of vision, the delight of inspirations and recollections. All synthesized into one experience. I could not separate my delight in reflecting on process-relational theology from my shoes hitting the pavement or the wind against my face in the totality of the Holy Here and Now. I couldn't discern which experience was most real – the rain or my body - and which most a part of me in the fullness of experience.

Whitehead's process-relational vision joins cosmological interdependence, the physiology of feeling and sensation, intellectual reflection, and spiritual insight. God is as real, Whitehead avers, in the secular as in the sacred. The secular is simply divinity in disguise, God hidden in the process of sensation and digestion, in gravity and planetary rotation. The sacred is the experience of the Holy within the wonder of our being and the wonder of all being. Divine energy inspires both cells and souls.

Eric Liddell runs and feels God's pleasure in pumping arms and legs. Annie Dillard experiences holiness as sun pierces the tree branches, giving birth to the "tree with lights." Mary Oliver finds holiness in the feel of the grass and breezes as she spends a "summer day" gazing on a grasshopper going about its business, hopping and

---

61   Ibid, 22-23.

chewing. Thomas Merton feels amazing love just looking at passers-by on a busy Louisville boulevard. We are thought and meditation, delight and wonder. We are also sense and emotion. The monk is all eye, so said a North African desert parent. When the doors of perception open, fully cleansed, to use the imagery of William Blake and Aldous Huxley, on a Cape Cod beach, we experience the infinity of all creation including our own moment by moment experiences.

We are soul energy. We are divine imagination in finite experience. We are a community of communities of cells, organs, emotions, inspirations, and thoughts. My friend and colleague Candace Pert (1946-2013) describes the "molecules of emotion" and asserts that the chemical interactions within our bodies form a dynamic and lively information network, linking mind and body. Our stomachs feel and our brains taste. Spirit is embodied and bodies are inspired in the intricate and intimate marriage of mind and body.

Our experience reflects the interconnectedness of the universe. Our sense of unity with the larger universe, the insight that our experience includes the whole universe, is the foundation of ethics and mysticism. "Love your neighbor as yourself" reflects the unity of myself and those around me. We rise from the same universe, synthesize many of the same data, and shape the future of ourselves and others by our moment-by-moment processes of self-creation. My future selves, in the flow of experience I call myself, share a common emergence with others' future selves. As I bring beauty and joy to my experience, I shape my future selves and the future selves of others. There is no separate "other" in experience, the relationship of mind and body, or our relationship with the wider world. Our self is the lively, dynamic, creative, and evolving center experience with which I identify as my own life. Yet, paranormal and mystical experiences join us with the intimate experiences of others. We experience a unity that breaks open the isolated, individualist, separate self.

Our personal center is here and it is also everywhere. Just as God is here and present everywhere. This is not pantheism, in which all is God, but what theologian and spiritual guide Jay McDaniel describes as "relational panentheism," in which I am in God, God is in me, and all things are in one another:

> the universe and God [are] within each other and thus parts of each other. The hills and rivers, trees and stars, and our feelings and decisions have their independence and integrity, even as God is also present in us and we in God. We call this relational panentheism."[62]

The dynamic unity of experience reflects the dynamic interdependence of the universe.

We are in process, but our process is the gift of relationships. We bring health to the world by identifying others with our deepest emotions, seeing their joy as our joy, their success as our success, their healing as our healing, their justice as our justice.

Experiencing Unity. Spirituality is sensational! When the doors of perception are opened and cleansed, we feel a unity with life, the inner and outer flow into each other. The barriers between mind and body, spirit and flesh, self and other, person and environment are broken down. There is no "other" separated from me. This is not pantheism, but spiritual spaciousness in which my center of experience is joined with all others in a symphony of creativity and compassion.

In this spiritual exercise, simply take time to experience the world around you without agenda. Be an aimlessly wandering monk, just noticing the feel of the earth, the joy of the senses. Experience life flowing into you. Relax into the universe as the outer and the inner are one. With beauty all around, let us walk and run and sit.

---

62 Jay McDaniel, "Panentheism: The Universe as God's Body," *Open Horizons*. Web.

28.

The basis of democracy is the common fact of value experience, as constituting the essential nature of each pulsation of actuality. Everything has some value for itself, for others, and for the whole. This characterizes the meaning of actuality. By reason of this character, constituting reality, the concept of morals arises. We have no right to deface the value experiences which is the very essence of the universe. Existence, in its very nature, is the upholding of value intensity.[63]

Cosmology, theology, ethics, spirituality, and politics are intimately connected in Whitehead's philosophy. Process-relational theology's vision of a dynamic, interdependent, value-oriented, and moral universe, guided by a relational, non-coercive God fosters a politics of diversity and compassion.

Cosmology shapes public policy and political perspectives. Interdependence breeds partnership and empathy. Affirming the universal aim toward intensity and complexity of experience promotes cooperation and advocacy in which our wellbeing and the wellbeing of others is connected. Dynamism inspires openness to change and willingness to question prior assumptions. Universal values, at every stage of human life and embracing human and non-human experience, inspires a politics of reverence. Theologies that see divine inspiration as ubiquitous and present in the "secular" as well as "spiritual" realms promote openness to scientific discovery. Theological positions that see God as non-authoritarian, relational, and non-coercive God give birth to non-coercive, relational, egalitarian political visions.

Whitehead is a philosopher of diversity and democracy. Democracy depends on affirming the universality of human value. Whatever has value deserves ethical and political consideration. Dehumanizing and disvaluing of certain humans is fundamental in economic and racial inequality. Privileging races, genders, sexual expressions, and nations of origin is connected with diminishing the

---

63 *Modes of Thought.*, 111.

values and worth of others. The "other" is a lesser mortal, differing from us in experience, emotions, and intellect. Those who proclaim that unique exceptionalism claim that lesser mortals do not deserve equal consideration in polling places, educational institutions, and economic opportunities.

Democracy depends on the affirmation that "everything has some value for itself, for others, and for the whole," characteristic of the meaning of actuality. Value for oneself means the ability to make decisions about one's life, live abundantly and fully and to have the opportunity to explore one's potential and vocation. Value for others means the ability to make a difference, to be given the opportunity to play a leadership role in one's community, and to bless others by your achievements. Value for the whole involves assuming one's role as a political actor, of moving from the polling place to political office to the presidency and vice-presidency. A healthy democracy promotes universal self-affirmation, agency, and activism. Community is healthy only when as many citizens as possible can be agents of their personal and political adventures. Accordingly, democracies must always be restless and forward looking as they seek a more perfect union.

Process-relational theology promotes a pragmatic progressivism. Healthy democracies depend on a vision of progress toward new perfections of justice, equality, and opportunity. Often, however, public policy must embrace the "best for that impasse." Not perfect or final, and always subject to revision, democracies are always restless and hopeful, expanding the circle of compassion, ethics, and political involvement to embrace the varied human communities as well as the non-human world.

Spirituality of Affirming Value. At the heart of a process-relational vision of democracy is the affirmation of value. Whatever exists has value, intrinsically and extrinsically. Whatever exists deserves our moral consideration. When a society chooses to devalue individuals based on race, sexuality, citizenship status, gender, physical or mental ability, and race, that society promotes disease in the body politic.

Wellbeing of persons, groups, and communities is interdependent. Perceptive process-relational persons value everyone and recognize those who are excluded from value, those whose lives are diminished by systemic injustice.

In this exercise, notice who is heard and who is silent, who is at the center and who is at the margins, who receives justice and who is treated unjustly in our society and also our circle of relationships and institutional lives. Notice the cost of injustice on those who experience it and the cost to the society. Notice the pain of injustice, feel the struggles and hopelessness, the fear and anxiety. Out of these feelings of empathy, make a commitment to feel pain, respond to pain, and challenge injustice so that all people experience God's wholeness in their social context.

29.

> *Philosophy begins in wonder. And, at the end, when phil-*
> *osophic thought has done its best the wonder remains. If you like*
> *to phrase it so, philosophical is mystical. For mysticism is direct*
> *insight into depths as yet unspoken. But the purpose of philosophy*
> *is to rationalize mysticism: not by explaining it away, but by the*
> *introduction of verbal characterizations rationally coordinated.*
> *Philosophy is akin to poetry, and both of them seek to express that*
> *ultimate good sense which we term civilization.* [64]

Whitehead roots himself in the grand philosophical tradition of the West, where philosophy aimed at wisdom, at seeing the big picture of life, and discerning where our lives fit in terms of values, ethics, and destiny. Whitehead was familiar with the words of Plato and Aristotle, respectively:

> "I see, my dear Theaetetus, that Theodorus had a true
> insight into your nature when he said that you were a philoso-
> pher, for wonder is the feeling of a philosopher, and philosophy
> begins in wonder."
> "It was their wonder, astonishment, that first led men to
> philosophize and still leads them."

In this penultimate day of "walking with Whitehead," I con-fess that these meditations could be described by the words of the spiritual, "I wonder as I wander out under the sky" on Cape Cod beaches on a month of mornings in the winter of the pandemic. Whitehead would have affirmed Rabbi Abraham Joshua Heschel's statement that the heart of religion is "radical amazement." I won-der as I wonder about many things, many of them unanswerable:

- Why is there something rather than nothing?
- Where does our notion of God come from?
- Why is there so much suffering in the world?
- Will justice and love prevail?

---

64   Ibid., 168, 174.

- Is my vision of God and faith aligned with the way things really are?
- When a friend of the same age dies, I wonder, why wasn't it me?
- Despite the personal and professional challenges I've faced, I wonder, why was I born in the USA with so much privilege while others are born in war torn, famine ridden nations? Will they receive justice and healing in the afterlife?
- Why must I die? Why must we die?
- Do I have a destiny beyond the grave?
- And in this day, when I announced my resignation as pastor of a beloved congregation, I wonder "what's next?" for me as a leave this holy place Cape Cod and return to another holy place, the suburbs of the USA Capitol.

Theologian Paul Tillich spoke of the "ontological shock of non-being," the recognition of the finitude and transitoriness of all things, and that the world could have been vastly different than what it is. What we take for granted is amazing and didn't have to be this way!

Wondering and wandering are at the heart of the spiritual journey and theological reflection. They are at the heart of what it means to evolve as a human. To look beyond the present moment to fathom the universe and to aspire to that generality of thought and vision that gives birth to morality, philosophy, theology, and world loyalty. That takes us beyond self to affirm the wellbeing of strangers and to devote our lives to being "good ancestors" for future generations.

Whitehead acknowledges that the mystical sources of religious experience take us beyond words. As Augustine confessed, if you think you know it, isn't God! We must trust the *kataphatic* way, the path of experience and encounter with the Holy and affirm that our symbols point to a deeper reality. We must also recognize that *apophatic* way, that all symbols are fingers pointing to the moon and not the moon itself and that all of our mystical experiences are time-bound, finite, and perspectival. We can experience the Holy, we can walk with God, but our experience is fully human. Even experiences of transcendence are rooted in time and space.

Philosophy and theology attempt to "rationalize mysticism," to understand and describe the mystical roots of religion. This rationalization is aimed at greater awareness rather than denial of the fundamental religious realities. Whitehead's vision of God as relational, creative and responsive, eternal and ever-changing, is an attempt to rationalize the highest intuitions of the Holy, where mysticism and ethics meet. Whiteheadian thought is never complete. Process-relational theology is always in process, but we believe that the moment we begin to describe our experiences of the Holy, we enter the realm of philosophical theology and ethics. We have experienced the Holy, but what "kind" of Holy do we experience? How does our experience of the Holy relate to the fundamental realities of day-to-day experience, culture, political policies, ethical intuitions, and the scientific adventure? Our encounter with God must in our time be framed in relationship to religious and cultural pluralism, physics and biology, evolution and the Big Bang, psychology and anthropology.

Still, the wonder remains and as our imaginations and experiences wander, we discover God within and God beyond, and a never ending cosmic adventure.

Cultivating Wonder. Psychiatrist Erik Erikson spoke of basic or primordial trust as essential to healthy living. Most of us need to rekindle basic trust as part of our spiritual maturity. We reclaim what we lost – or never received – as fetuses, infants, and toddlers. The same applies to wonder and radical amazement. The child lives in a magic reality. The neonate comes to earth trailing clouds of glory. Over the years, life becomes routine and manageable and we lose the sense of wonder. Boredom, dullness, repetition replace novelty and adventure. We can't go back to our childhoods chronologically or experientially, but we can go forward to new possibilities of living in the Holy Here and Holy Now and the Holy Future that awaits us. As the group of my youth, the Byrds sang, "every day can be a magic carpet ride."

Cultivating wonder involves again opening to our experience of the world. Opening our senses to the world around us. Opening our mind to the spirit within us. Being all sense and all intuition. As you begin each day, pray to look more deeply into life. Pray that you receive divine messages as you go through the day. Ask for an open heart and open senses. Then throughout the day pause in every encounter, phone call, interruption, even if more a second to notice.

Begin and end the day gazing at the heavens. Look for God-moments in scudding clouds, birds flying overhead, random conversations, music, intuitions, the voices of friends and strangers.

Give thanks throughout the day for the simple wonder of your being and the amazing world in which we live.

30.

The final outlook of Philosophic thought cannot be based upon the exact statements which form the basis of special sciences. The exactness is a fake.[65]

We conclude our meditations with a call to humility. In a lively, dynamic, ever-flowing universe, finality is a phantasm. Evolution is emerging and history is open-ended. Dogmatism, whether in politics or religion, is ultimately dangerous. Dogmatic theologians and ideological politicians believe that disagreement and diversity are threats to be eliminated. From their perspective, variety must be suppressed in favor of uniformity of belief and behavior. Prophets must be silenced to maintain the status quo and their privilege. Homogeneity is preferred over diversity.

In reality, the affirmation that any of us have metaphysical, political, and theological exactness is not only fake; it is also false and small-spirited. Exactness sees God here and not there. Dogmatic certainty affirms truth in your community but not others and discovers God in our sacraments but not in others' rituals.

There is a virtue in vagueness in the spiritual journey. Too much exactness and clarity privileges our viewpoints while denying the value of others' insights. Too much clarity leads to prizing abstractions rather than concrete experience. Faith is first experiential and then doctrinal. Real spirituality, like real life, is messy, unpredictable, and constantly in flux. Real politics is not for the faint-hearted: as the saying goes, it's like making sausage – the result may be tasty but the process is disgusting. Life is complicated. Life takes us beyond the binary world of saved and unsaved, male and female, friend and foe, nation and planet, and black and white.

Spiritual evolution nurtures Bodhisattvas and Mahatmas whose vision is wide as the skies. Jesus never stays put intellectually or spiritually but grows in wisdom and stature. Beyond exactness and narrowness is the adventure of the spirit, captured by Patricia

---

65   Alfred North Whitehead, "Immortality," Section XIX.

Adams Farmer as the "fat soul" and Bernard Loomer as "S-I-Z-E, " a largeness of spirit that embraces otherness and contrast with intellectual and relational hospitality and integrity.

WALKING FORWARD

We began our walk with Whitehead focusing on moving from self-interest to world and from small spiritedness to global consciousness. When I began this walk on New Year's Day 2021, I did not know that I would be physically moving and leaving a beloved community with no clear professional path ahead. I trust that my future will be found in the walking!

Process-relational theology aims at producing persons and institutions of stature and cosmopolitan spirit, mirroring God's love that joins the universal and particular and infinite and intimate. We seek the truth and recognize our limitations. We can experience the Divine as a living reality, but our descriptions of the Holy are always finite and perspectival. God's Holy Adventure embodied in the great spiritual teachers and calling us forward joins the joy of the present and the restless quest for the future. The walk forward we will continue to "love the questions," remember our mortality and our infinite spirit, and live by the prophetic counsel:

> He has told you, O mortal, what is good;
> and what does the Lord require of you
> but to do justice, and to love mercy,
> and to walk humbly with your God? (Micah 6:8)

An Exercise in Openness. In this exercise, prayerfully and without judgment look back on the certainties of your childhood, youth, and adulthood. Which ones have stood the test of time and relationship? Which have you discarded in favor of better understandings of life or because you found them wanting? What did you gain by letting go of previous certainties?

Now, looking at your current life. Are there any certainties that you are examining or that are under attack by others? What new possibilities are stretching you physically or spiritually? What new personal prospects are creating both anticipation and anxiety? How do you feel about the prospect of letting go of these? What will be lost and what will be gained?

In your imagination, place your certainties and uncertainties in God's care. Open to new truths that may come to you with gratitude for a larger vision of life. In the spirit of process-relational thought, make a commitment to share in God's adventures of ideas, embracing God's vision of your life and the world.

+++

Process-relational theo-spirituality is a Holy Adventure. Let us go forth humbly and adventurously, not knowing what the future will bring, but trusting that God will give us the vision we need to live joyfully and bring beauty to the earth, living the insights of process-relational theology in our personal and professional lives, relationships, and citizenship. Let us trust intuition, mysticism, and synchronicity along with reason and analysis. Let us walk humbly, justly, and imaginatively with God as our Companion, Challenger, Guide, and Beloved Pilgrim.

CPSIA information can be obtained
at www.ICGtesting.com
Printed in the USA
JSHW010307030223
37220JS00003B/85